Making
Fine Wines
and
Liqueurs
at
Home

by LEIGH P. BEADLE

BREW IT YOURSELF
MAKING FINE WINES AND
    LIQUEURS AT HOME

Making Fine Wines and Liqueurs at Home

LEIGH P. BEADLE

FARRAR, STRAUS AND GIROUX
NEW YORK

To my wife, Becky, and to my mother

ACKNOWLEDGMENT

I would like to express my appreciation to the research depart-
ments of the various wineries, to the yeast experimentation
laboratories of the major yeast-producing firms, and to the
Wine Institute for their technical assistance in writing this book.

COPYRIGHT NOTICE

CONTENTS

Who loves not wine, woman and song
Remains a fool his whole life long.

—Anonymous

Making Fine Wines and Liqueurs at Home

Author's Note

During the past few years there has been a tremendous increase in the number of people who have taken up the hobby of home wine making. This popularity is due to the greater amount of leisure time now available to many people and to their desire to fill this time with unique and interesting diversions from the routine of daily life. As wine makers' supply outlets began to proliferate and literature on the subject—mainly from England and Canada —began appearing on bookshelves, people became aware that this art, once the exclusive domain of professional vintners and monastic monks, could be enjoyed by anyone who had the desire to turn out fine wine.

Until recently, home wine making required much time and considerable expense because bushels of grapes had to be mashed in grape crushers to extract the juices. Even the smaller crushers cost over eighty dollars, and the price of the grapes themselves pushed the cost of making wines at home above that of buying even some of the best domestic brands. With all this, there was still the all-too-frequent chance of failure due to inferior grapes or to wild yeasts taking over the ferment. With recent advances in the wine industry, it is now possible to make an excellent wine at home with very little initial expense and no chance of a spoiled batch. The reason for this great advance in home wine making is the development by several of the distinguished wineries in California of grape concentrates made specifically for wine making. Don't be misled by the term "concentrate." These bear no relation to the grape concentrates on grocers' shelves which are used for making grape juice. The wine-making concentrates are the pure juices of the *vinifera* wine grape only, with the addition of a sterilizing solution used by all wineries here and abroad to inhibit the growth of wild yeasts. These concentrates, used for years by the major wineries to improve the quality of their wines and provide uniformity of taste from year to year, are now available for the home wine maker. They greatly reduce initial cost because expensive grape-crushing equipment is no longer needed. Also, the cost of the concentrate itself is much less than the cost of buying several bushels of grapes—around ten dollars for enough concentrate to make a five-gallon batch of wine, or twenty-five bottles. That works out to less than fifty cents a bottle for wine that is equal or superior to the most expensive domestic brands and which, I feel, compares favorably with imported wines from France. A complete fermentation kit for five-gallon batches, designed to last a lifetime, is available for less than twenty dollars, including shipping. To make this book a foolproof guide for the home wine maker, all ingredients and their sources are listed by brand name. This book was written expressly for the American public and all items are available domestically.

A note on the legal status of home wine making. Under the present laws, you can make up to two hundred gallons of wine a year for your own consumption and that of your family. (That's almost three bottles a day, more than enough for even the most immoderate imbiber!) You cannot sell it, nor can you transport it out of your house, so if you want to stay within the technical bounds of the law, you will have to invite friends over if you want them to sample it. You must also obtain Form 1541 from your assistant regional commissioner of the Internal Revenue Service. This is simply a permit to make wine at home and it costs nothing.

A unique feature of this book is a complete section on making liqueurs at home. This is a new field which is rapidly attracting the attention of home wine hobbyists in this country. Extracts for making liqueurs have been available to Europeans for over fifty years. They are made by a firm in France and are now available in this country. Over forty different types are available, including every kind found commercially in liquor stores. The initial reaction from people who first become aware of these extracts is that they couldn't possibly turn out as good a product as the commercial variety. The truth is that the end product is as good as the store-bought variety and, in some cases, considerably better, depending on the particular flavor. Liqueurs can be mixed in less than ten minutes and require no aging. The cost is less than four dollars a fifth to make. The cost of the commercial varieties ranges from four to ten dollars a fifth, depending on the type. It is also entirely legal to make liqueurs at home, since you are buying the alcohol base—vodka—from a store. At least I hope you will buy the vodka and not try to make it yourself, or you'll be in trouble!

A final note for those of you who have visions of large vessels, pipes, and odoriferous airs permeating your home or apartment. Using the equipment and simple procedures detailed in this book, you will need no more space than is required for a large wastebasket. A small corner of a room or even a closet is sufficient. The equipment weighs less than six pounds, is designed to be used at standard room temperatures, and will not produce any objectionable odors. Your wife (or husband) being sufficiently reassured, you are now ready to indulge successfully in what was once the art of only the truly anointed.

Glossary of
Wine-Making Terms

ACID BLEND

A blend of three fruit acids — citric, malic, and tartaric — usually
in equal amounts. Used in wine making to raise the acid level
of the mix to the correct level and to provide a slight tart taste
to the wine.

ACETIC ACID

The chemical formed by acetic bacteria, causing wine to turn
to vinegar. These bacteria can only survive in air and are therefore no problem when the entire fermentation is anaerobic or
without air.

AEROBIC FERMENTATION

Old method of fermentation in which wine was exposed for
long periods to the air. A prime cause of spoilage.

ANAEROBIC FERMENTATION

Type of fermentation, used in this book, in which air is ex-
cluded to prevent any chance of spoilage or oxidation of the
wine.

ASCORBIC ACID
Pure vitamin C. Used in wine making at the rate of one half teaspoon to five gallons prior to bottling to prevent oxidation.

BODY
Term used to describe the fullness of wines.

BOUQUET
The pleasant and distinctive aroma given off by a fine wine, contributing greatly to its enjoyment.

CAMPDEN TABLETS
Bisulphite in tablet form used at the rate of two four-gram tablets per gallon to sterilize the grape mix and kill all undesirable wild yeast. Some grape concentrates are pre-bisulphited at the winery, in which case the tablets must not be used since they will kill the wine yeast.

CARBON DIOXIDE
The gas produced by the reproduction of yeast. The action of the yeast converts grape sugar and other sugars into carbon dioxide gas and alcohol in approximately equal amounts.

CARBOY
The secondary fermenter. A closed polyethylene container in which the anaerobic fermentation of the wine takes place.

DEPOSITS
The pulp and other sediment which settle just above the pure yeast layer when using raw fruits to make wine. These deposits do not form when using pure concentrates. Among wine makers these deposits are also called "lees."

DEXTROSE
Also called corn sugar. Sometimes used as a substitute by weight for household sugar in wine making. Tends to give a slightly smoother taste to some lighter wines.

FERMENTATION
Process by which yeast acts on sugar to convert it to carbon dioxide gas and alcohol in approximately equal amounts.

FERMENTATION LOCK
Also called an air lock. A device to ensure that carbon dioxide gas can escape from the carboy without allowing air to enter.

FININGS
Used in wine making to produce a brilliantly clear wine. Gelatin is one of the best fining agents.

FORTIFICATION
Adding spirits—usually grain alcohol or brandy—to wine to increase the alcohol content beyond that attainable through natural fermentation.

GELATIN
See FININGS.

HYDROMETER
A device used by wine makers to measure the sugar content in the wine mix. Also called a saccharometer.

INVERT SUGAR
Similar to dextrose.

ISINGLASS
A fining agent made from the bladder of sturgeon, once used extensively. Not as effective as gelatin finings.

LEES
See DEPOSITS.

LIQUOR
The unfermented grape mix prior to the addition of yeast.

MALO-LACTIC FERMENTATION
The third fermentation that takes place in wine making, mellowing the wine and giving it character.

MALO-LACTIC GASES
The slight gases which form during the malo-lactic fermentation. They must be totally dispelled before the wine can become smooth.

MUST
A term for the unfermented wine mix.

NUTRIENT
An essential additive in wine making which ensures that the yeast will carry on a vigorous ferment.

PRIMARY FERMENTER
A vessel which contains the wine mix during the initial tumultuous fermentation.

RACKING
The practice of transferring the wine from one carboy to another by siphoning it off the yeast layer. This is necessary only in a prolonged fermentation to prevent the yeast layer from affecting the wine.

SACCHAROMETER
See HYDROMETER.

SACCHAROMYCES ELLIPSOIDEUS
Latin name for pure wine yeast.

SECONDARY FERMENTER
Also called a carboy. Vessel in which the anaerobic fermentation takes place.

SIPHONING
Method by which liquid is transferred from one container to another. For siphoning to take place, the pouring end of the hose must be lower than the suction end.

SPECIFIC GRAVITY
The scale used to determine the sugar content of the wine mix. This scale assumes water to have a gravity of 1.000 at 60° F.

TANNIN
Substance found in red wines and to a lesser extent in white wines. Gelatin works in conjunction with the tannin to clear the wine.

TARTARIC ACID
A fruit acid formed in the grape.

WINE
That delightful beverage, which, along with LIQUEURS, is what this book is all about.

YEAST
Simple, one-celled organisms which reproduce rapidly in sugary solutions, such as grape mix, and whose bacchanalian activities in these mixes give rise to the production of higher alcohols.

History of Wine Making

Wine making is an art which has its origins in the dawn of civilization. Botanical data indicate that the wine grapes of today are descended from older species found in the mountains of Armenia, located south of the Caucasus. Archaeological records show that the cultivation of grape vineyards, known as viticulture, probably began in that region and spread to Mesopotamia over five thousand years ago. Wine was a luxury available only to the wealthy in Mesopotamia, as it had to be imported great distances from the highlands, where the soil was more amenable to the growing of grapes.

Wine making spread to Egypt, where the vines thrived in the rich soil and climate. On tombs, dating as far back as the first dynasty (ca. 3000 B.C.) are depictions of the dead lying on a bed of grapes which accompany them on their journey. The vineyards gradually spread along the

Nile Delta to Memphis. Records show that the grapes were pressed by treading them with bare feet and the juices fermented in cool cellars. The Egyptians began the custom of classifying wine. They had inspectors who judged the quality of wine, and the pottery containers had inscriptions bearing details of the vintage: the name of the vineyard, the date of harvest and pressing, the name of the vintner, and the brand. The Egyptians were also the first to try to improve their various brands of wine by blending them with the grapes from other regions, notably Palestine and Syria. Even with the Egyptians' penchant for scientific experimentation and blending, however, we know from the ancient authors of the period that their wines were inferior to those produced in Syria and Palestine. It is interesting to note that in all these countries the wine was always diluted with water before it was consumed. Since these areas had poor drinking water, this custom probably developed more from a need to improve the water than from a desire to weaken the wine.

Viticulture spread to the Aegean Sea around 1500 B.C. The Greeks were quick to learn the techniques developed by the Egyptians and improved on them with their own botanical discoveries. They even came to the conclusion that it was not the Egyptian god Osiris but the Greek god Dionysus who made the first grapes. The Greeks must be credited with a major advance in the art of wine making by their development of the beam press, used in separating the juice from the grape. Theretofore, the primary method of collecting the juices for making white wine was the use of a wringer developed by the Egyptians. It was a rather bulky arrangement consisting of a large fabric bag suspended from a support. The bag would be filled with grapes and wrung out by turning a long wooden rod inserted through the bottom, thus squeezing the juice from the grapes. The Greek press worked more on the principle of a standard wine press. The Greeks developed vessels for transporting their wines, which were coated with resin or bitumen on the inside to render them nonporous. These substances gave the wine a peculiar flavor, for which the Greeks acquired a taste and which is still evident in their retsina, or resinated wine. They credited wine with many medicinal properties, and a large portion of the various healing potions used by Greek physicians had a grape wine base.

The Romans were avid practitioners of the art of viticulture and seemed to imbibe as eagerly as the Greeks. Graphic evidence of this is a hill in Rome, 150 feet high, called Mount Testaccia, which consists entirely of broken wine jars! The Romans carried the art of wine making to all the territories they conquered, notably present-day France, Spain, and Germany. They invented the screw press, which was more efficient than the Greek beam press and was the most common type of press used up to the present time. The Romans were also able to create a hardier species of grapevine which could withstand frost. They grew these grapes along the banks of the Moselle and the Rhine. When the Roman Empire declined and the widespread wine industry was destroyed during the barbarian invasions, the Church protected and carried on viticulture, although only on a small scale. Wine was used as a sacrament at all Church rituals, and wherever a new church was built, a vineyard was planted. Since wine was not made for profit, the emphasis was on quality rather than quantity.

England had a limited wine industry around the eighth century, as indicated by some of the writings of the Venerable Bede (probably a distant ancestor of the Venerable Beadle). By the ninth century, the landed gentry and nobility along with the churches were actively engaged in viticulture. After the Norman Conquest, the number of English vineyards greatly increased. However, when the English subsequently acquired a vast amount of French territory, including the huge vineyards of the Bordeaux region in southwestern France, they diminished considerably because the British preferred the imported French wine to their own home-grown variety. The French could easily produce enough wine for England's needs, and over the next three hundred years the vineyards of England were destroyed and other crops planted in their place. In the meantime, the wine-producing areas of France became larger and more efficient in their production. Charlemagne, in the eighth century, is credited with planting the Burgundian vineyards, which continue to produce some of the world's finest wines. The Benedictine monk, Dom Pérignon, did extensive experiments with blending various grape varieties in the seventeenth century. Spanish sherry became the popular wine in England in the sixteenth century, followed by port in the eighteenth century. In the latter part of the nineteenth century, the vineyards of Europe were ravaged by the accidental importation of a small, parasitic louse from America called *Phylloxera vastatrix*. The American vines were resistant to this scourge, but the European vines were devastated by the pest, which burrowed into the roots of the grapevines and consumed them. After much experimentation, it was found that by grafting grapevine roots from American vineyards to the European vines, the vineyards were rendered immune to this destructive parasite.

Wine Making in the United States

America was recognized quite early in its history as a potential wine-making country when Leif Ericson and his Norse crew stepped ashore. After noting the proliferation of native grapes growing in the virgin forests with vines climbing to the tops of the trees, he proclaimed this newly discovered land Vinland, or "Wineland," a phrase used in Norse literature for centuries to describe America. Indeed, there was an abundance of grapevines in America, none of them the European *Vitis vinifera*, however. Of the many native American species, the most prominent were the *Vitis riparia*, *Vitis labrusca*, and *Vitis rotundifolia*, the last being used to make the distinctly American scuppernong wine.

Wine making in the United States developed along two different geographical lines. The English, in the seventeenth century, tried to make a palatable wine using native grapes. Captain John Smith was one of the first to try to tame the American grape. In his diary he wrote:

Of vines, great abundance in many parts, that climbe the toppes of trees in some places, but these beare but few grapes except by the rivers and savage habitations, where they are overshadowed from the sunne, they are covered with fruit though never prunned nor manured. Of these hedge grapes we made neere twentie gallons of wine, which was like our British wine, but certainly they would prove good were they well manured.

The English failed in their early attempts at using native grapes, so they tried to cultivate cuttings of the *Vitis vinifera*. These attempts continued for two hundred years, but the European wine grape was not able to acclimate to the rigors of soil and climate on the East Coast, and, unknown to the growers, was susceptible to the infestations of the Phylloxera plant louse.

In the latter part of the eighteenth century, viticulturists turned their efforts to domesticating native grapes, and this led finally to the successful development of American grape varieties. These were crossbred and domesticated for wine making. Among the types developed were the Delaware, scuppernong, Catawba, Niagara, and Concord, the last being the most commonly used. These wines have a distinctly different flavor from the European grape wines, with a spicy character and aroma all their own. Wine industries developed in the Eastern and Midwestern states using these varieties.

The California wine industry developed quite apart from that on the East Coast. Just twenty-six years after

Columbus made his first voyage to America, Cortez, the Spanish explorer, ordered that wine making become an industry in the New World. He stipulated that certain landholders must plant, for five years, one thousand vines for every one hundred Indians living on the land in Mexico and lower California. These were European grapevines from Spain. Unlike the vines imported to the East Coast, the newly planted grapes thrived in the California soil and climate. The cultivation of the vineyards was carried on by the Franciscans, who extended them into upper California, where the climate and soil were even more ideal. The Franciscans did not develop wine making on a commercial scale, however. Their wine was used more for sacramental table use and for treating the sick.

It was not until the early nineteenth century that commercial growers began to settle in California. Within a generation, wine making was the principal industry in the Los Angeles area. With prosperity in the industry came improvements in the wine. Cuttings were brought from France to improve the vineyards and to increase the varieties.

Unfortunately, the use of the delicate European vines led to disaster later on. The dreaded Phylloxera plant louse found its way to California, probably on some infested cuttings brought back from Europe, and laid waste most of the vineyards. When it was found that grafting the roots of the native Eastern American grapevines to the European varieties in California and overseas rendered the plants immune to the Phylloxera, the scourge was arrested. The California wine industry was rebuilt, and its wines began receiving worldwide recognition for their quality until a worse scourge struck them in 1919. This disaster, worse than the vilest plague, was called Prohibition. Many vineyards were destroyed and other crops planted in their place during the thirteen years of prohibition. Some vineyards did survive, however, due in part to the demand for grapes by individuals who could still legally make, at home, up to two hundred gallons of wine a year for their own consumption. This is the same law which applies to our own home wine making. Following the repeal of prohibition, it was many years before the wine industry reached its former output in both quantity and quality. Stringent quality standards were enacted to encourage wineries to maintain high standards, so that, today, American wines are once again earning the praise of connoisseurs the world over.

How Wine Is Made Commercially

The procedure for making wines at home is quite similar to the method used by commercial wineries, although some of the initial steps, such as pressing grapes and blending the juices, are no longer required by the home wine maker due to the development of grape concentrates made specifically for home wine production. This section will give a good insight into the techniques involved in making wines and how we parallel these with our own procedures.

The prime determinant of the final quality of the wine is the quality of the grape itself. While there are many species of grapes grown in the world, only a very few are suitable for making wine. The most common grape used for wine making is the European *Vitis vinifera*, the predominant species grown in the vineyards of California. The vineyards are cultivated throughout the year. Between five hundred and eight hundred vines are grown on each acre. Four years are required to bring new vineyards to their full bearing potential, and they require more supervision than any other major crop. The grapes are harvested in late summer and transported to the winery for pressing while they are still fresh. Mechanical crushers are used to separate the stems from the grapes. This is necessary because the stems contain large amounts of tannin, which would cause the wine to taste bitter if left in the juice. The crusher then presses the grapes with enough force to open them and release the juices but lightly enough so that the seeds are not crushed. The seeds also contain tannin, which would affect the flavor. A small amount of tannin is released during the fermentation process; however, the quantity is such that it enhances the flavor and aids in clarification. When the grapes have been crushed, the pulp and juices are pumped into fermenters.

At this point, sulphur dioxide is added to the "must," as this juice is called. The amount added is very small, about seventy-five parts per million, but this is enough to sterilize the must. This is a very important process in the making of good wine. The skins of grapes carry a powdery cover called the "bloom." This is composed of molds and many types of wild yeasts, including *Saccharomyces ellipsoideus*, the true wine yeast. In wine making, it is desirable to kill all these wild yeasts by sterilization with the sulphur dioxide and then to inoculate the must with a yeast culture composed only of a pure selected strain of *Saccharomyces ellipsoideus*. The wineries maintain carefully nurtured colonies of this yeast to ensure a complete and consistent fermentation. It was found long ago that if the grapes were allowed to ferment from the action of their own wild yeasts, the process was more sluggish and often incomplete. The reason for this is that the wild yeasts could not tolerate a high concentration of alcohol and would sometimes become inactive when the alcohol content reached 8 or 9 percent. The cultured yeast strains were developed for their ability to tolerate up to 15 percent alcohol before they died in their own by-product. These yeast cultures are also able to withstand the sterilizing effect of the sulphur dioxide, and the process of fermentation is started. The yeast, which is a one-celled organism, multiplies by dividing itself and growing in the must. The yeast feeds on the grape sugar which is in the juices. Ripe wine grapes contain between 12 and 24 percent grape sugar by weight, 70 to 85 percent water, and a small amount of acids and minerals which give the grape, and hence the wine, its particular character. As the yeast consumes the sugar and multiplies, it forms alcohol and carbon dioxide gas in approximately equal amounts.

The process of fermentation takes from several days to several weeks, depending on the percentage of sugar in the must, the temperature, and the strain of wine yeast being used. In modern-day wineries, the fermenting vats are fitted with cooling coils to maintain an even temperature during fermentation. Temperature control is required when large quantities of wine are being fermented since the process generates heat. After the primary fermentation is completed, the wine is transferred to secondary fermenters, or storage tanks. The juice is pumped from the primary fermenting vat, and the crushed grape pulps are left behind. It is at this point that a grape press is used for the first time. Note that in the beginning the grapes were only lightly crushed. Now the leftover pulps are squeezed to extract all the remaining juices. This wine, if left separate from the juices previously pumped from the vat, is called press wine. The other is referred to as free run wine.

The wine ages in the storage tanks for a period of time, usually several weeks, during which it begins to clear and sediment slowly accumulates on the bottom of the tanks. These deposits are known as "lees." If the wine rests too long on the lees, the flavor will be altered to some degree. For this reason, the wine is periodically transferred off the lees to another tank. This process is called racking, and it is repeated several times during the aging of the wine. During this period, the wine is occasionally blended with other wine or with concentrates to maintain a uniformity in taste from batch to batch.

Wine is also made brilliantly clear during the aging process, either by filtration or by the use of fining agents. This is necessary because there are usually microscopic particles of fruit or chemical matter in suspension which, if not removed, would give the wine a hazy or cloudy appearance. If the wine is filtered, it is run through several pads with varying degrees of porosity. The suspended particles are trapped in the filters as the wine passes through them. Some filters are fine enough to trap microscopic yeast cells and prevent further fermentation. Certain wine experts claim that the taste of the wine is diminished somewhat by filtration, although others claim just as avidly that there is no effect at all. In fining, the other method of clearing the wine, the most common agents used by the wineries are bentonite or gelatin. Bentonite is a natural, claylike material which swells up in liquid and slowly settles to the bottom, carrying suspended particles with it. It is the most common fining agent used in American wineries. Gelatin, an organic agent, combines with tannin in the wine to form a colloid solution, which also settles to the bottom along with suspended matter. In some European wineries the whites of eggs are still used as a fining agent, although this practice became largely obsolete following the turn of the century.

During the time the wine is aging and clearing in the storage tanks, it is in an anaerobic environment, or one without air. There is still a residual amount of fermentation in progress, and the carbon dioxide gas thus formed escapes through air locks or low pressure valves which prevent air from entering. Any air that may be present in the tanks after the various rackings is forced out by the formation of carbon dioxide, which protects the wine. Most of the spoilage organisms, such as acetic bacteria which can turn wine to vinegar, are airborne and cannot survive in an anaerobic environment. Another reason for protecting the wine from long exposure to air is that it will oxidize. When wine oxidizes, it darkens and may become cloudy. The taste is also affected. The wine then cannot be saved by either filtration or fining. One of the prime causes of spoilage of wines made at home is oxidation from the use of incorrect fermenters. That problem is eliminated in this book.

The final step in commercial production prior to actual bottling is fast heating and cooling of the wine. This is done to deactivate certain enzymes which would otherwise discolor the wine in the bottle. This process is not to be confused with pasteurization, which is seldom used today due to the sterilization technique of adding sulphur dioxide and the use of pure yeast cultures. After the wine is bottled, it is aged for a period of time to allow it to mellow and reach its peak flavor. Wine is one of the few beverages that improves after bottling. Generally speaking, white wines reach their peak within a year or two of bottling, while some red wines require several years. Many California wines are at their best within a year of bottling and should be consumed during that time period. It is interesting to note that white wines can be made with either white or red grapes. Only the skins of grapes are colored. If you've ever peeled a grape (or, much better yet, had someone else peel one for you), you would have noticed that the inside of either a red or white grape is the same color. To make white wine the grape juice is separated from the skins just after it is crushed so that the skin coloring does not have a chance to affect the wine. To make red wine, both the skins and pulp are fermented with the juice to extract the coloring and flavors. This is one reason why red wine is generally more full-bodied in flavor than white wine.

Equipment for Home Wine Making

It is very important to have the right equipment when taking up the art of making wine at home. Using the correct equipment and following the simple procedures in the recipe sections, you can reasonably expect your first batch of wine to be as good as my last one. When hobbyists first take up wine making, they generally make one of two mistakes: they either pay too little for their equipment and wind up with faulty material, or they pay too much and end up with more than is necessary to produce a superior wine. One person I talked to recently spent over $250 for a wine press and oak barrels, not realizing that neither of these items is needed. On the other hand, I don't recommend using the types of wine kits offered by some stores which use thin, collapsible plastic bags for fermenters. These are hard to handle without billowing the yeast layer during fermentation, and the threaded air locks often allow the passage of air into the fermenter.

Your initial expense will be recouped during your first batch, even when adding the cost of the grape concentrate, normally under ten dollars. You will turn out twenty-five bottles of wine per batch, and even if you considered it worth only two dollars a bottle, that's fifty dollars worth of wine! Most people, however, consider the wine to be equal to that costing over twice as much. After your first batch, your only recurring expense will be the concentrate and additives. At a time when the prices of domestic and imported wines are skyrocketing, the average cost of producing your own bottle of good wine will be modest indeed.

Following is a description of a home fermentation kit.

PRIMARY FERMENTER

The container in which the ingredients are mixed and the primary, or tumultuous, fermentation takes place. Some people use stone crocks or large glass bottles for the primary fermenter, but these should be avoided. The crocks are hard to clean, and cleanliness is extremely important in quality wine making. Also, both crocks and glass containers are heavy and difficult to handle; if dropped there can be painful consequences. The primary fermenter used in the standard kit is rigid, inert polyethylene which will impart no taste to the wine. Polyethylene is also very easy to keep clean. It has a seven-gallon capacity to allow for the initial foamy head on the five-gallon mix. See Figure 1 following page 36.

SECONDARY FERMENTER

Also called a carboy. It is a closed, high-density poly-ethylene container with a capacity of 5½ gallons. This is the container in which the secondary, or anaerobic, fermentation takes place. The anaerobic fermentation guarantees quality batches each time, with no chance of spoilage. See Figure 2.

FERMENTATION LOCK

A plastic air lock attached to a pure gum-rubber stopper which is designed to fit the secondary fermenter. See Figure 3. This device ensures that carbon dioxide gas can escape from the carboy without letting in any air, since prolonged contact with air at this stage could spoil the wine by oxidation or contamination by acetic bacteria. You may ask at this point, "Why is it necessary to use the primary fermenter, why not just carry on the entire fermentation in the secondary fermenter?" The answer is that in the closed secondary fermenter, the initial foaming head would rise up through the fermentation lock and seep over the sides of the container onto the floor.

SIPHON UNIT

Used to transfer the wine from one container to another, and finally into the bottles. If the wine is simply poured from one vessel to another, the yeast layer on the bottom would billow. Figure 4 shows the principle of siphoning in which the flow end is lower than the drawing end. The ideal flow rate is achieved when the upper vessel is about twenty-one inches from the floor. This ingenious unit finally makes bottling a one-man operation, as it has the openings just above yeast layer height on the drawing end so that no one has to hold it carefully above the yeast. The practical method of cutting off the flow between bottles is shown in Figure 5.

THE HYDROMETER

A handy little instrument which we use to take all the guesswork out of wine making. It is a device used to measure the quantity of sugar in wine prior to fermentation. It also tells when fermentation is completed. Figure 6 shows a hydrometer similar to the type included in the standard wine fermentation kit. Wine hydrometers generally have three scales on the stem: the specific gravity scale, the balling scale, and the percent of alcohol scale. The specific gravity and the balling scales are two different gauges which tell us the same thing, but we will concern ourselves with only the specific gravity scale. It has smaller graduations for accuracy and is easier to use. The alcohol scale is simply a rough guide to the final percentage of alcohol in the wine. This is determined by the initial amount of sugar in the mix prior to the onset of fermentation. (More on this later.) The specific gravity scale assumes that pure distilled water at 60° F. has a weight or specific gravity reading of 1.000. If sugar, which is heavier than water, is added in solution, the hydrometer will float higher in the liquid and the scale will indicate a higher reading. Note that the hydrometer on the left in Figure 6 indicates a reading of 1.082. This, incidentally, is the approximate weight of the wine mix prior to fermentation when using the procedures in this book. A wine mix containing this amount of grape juice and sugar will produce a wine with an alcohol content of approximately 12 percent by volume, an ideal amount for fine wines.

Many years ago, prior to the invention of the hydrometer, wine making was a much more complicated procedure, as it took long experience, a very skillful eye, and a sophisticated palate to determine the correct consistency of the grape mix. The hydrometer makes it possible to instantly and accurately ascertain this. It is also a reliable gauge for determining when fermentaion is completed. All we have to know is what the final specific gravity of a particular wine should be after fermentation is finished. For example, most of the wines in this book will have a final gravity of .993 to .995. The hydrometer on the right in Figure 6 shows a reading of .995. By simply testing the wine after the normal fermentation period has ended, we can tell whether the fermentation is complete or whether the wine should remain in the carboy a little longer. A reading of .995 is less than the weight of water because the wine at this point has an alcohol content.

Alcohol is lighter than water; therefore, the hydrometer will float deeper than 1.000. Thus, to be fully functional for wine making, the hydrometer should have a scale with a lower limit of .990. The upper scale should go to 1.120 to give a range of 130. Most hydrometers have a range from .990 to 1.160, which is much higher than is really needed but in actual usage presents no problem.

You will notice that at the 1.082 level of the hydrometer, the corresponding alcohol percent scale shows a potential alcohol content of only approximately 11 percent. As I mentioned earlier, the actual percentage of alcohol in our wines will be 12 percent. The reason for the apparent discrepancy in the alcohol percent scale is that the scale begins at 1.000, the weight of water. If the wines worked out to only 1.000, as with ports and sherries, the scale would show a correct reading for alcohol content. Since the regular wines will work out to about .994, we will end up with an additional one percent alcohol from that indicated on the scale. It is, therefore, necessary only to add one to whatever reading we get on the alcohol scale to make it accurate for the regular wines. For those of you who enjoy mathematical formulas, we can complicate this simple instrument with a formula which allows us to accurately determine in advance the final alcohol content of our wines using only the specific gravity scale. Just figure the range of specific gravity between the initial gravity and the final gravity; in the regular wines this will usually be 88. ($1.082 - .994 = 88$.) You then divide this by the factor 7.36. (7.36 on the specific gravity scale is equal to one percent alcohol.) $88 \div 7.36 = 11.96$, or approximately 12 percent alcohol by volume. The factor

7.36 is constant for any fermented beverage when using specific gravity. All this information is academic, however. In case you are beginning to visualize wine making as a complex science, let me reassure you that all you really need to know about the hydrometer is how to read the initial and final specific gravity.

BOTTLES

Using the standard home fermentation kit you will produce enough wine to fill twenty-five "fifths," meaning bottles that hold four-fifths of a quart. This is the ideal size bottle for home wine making and the most easily attainable. Do not use quart bottles. These are too large for the decanting procedure which will be mentioned later. Before you start conjuring up images of expensive corking machines, corks, wires, and capsules, rest assured that you will require none of these. In fact, corks are highly undesirable for home wine making. (They are not the best method of sealing commercial wine bottles either, but try telling the French that!) For corks to provide an airtight seal, they have to be kept moist, which means the bottles must be stored on their sides. Home-made wine should be stored upright to allow the slight trace of yeast to settle to a film on the bottom of the bottle. The two best methods of bottling are in standard-size champagne bottles with plastic corks, or standard wine bottles with screw tops. These closures do not have to be moist to remain airtight, and since these bottles are nonreturnable, they are easy to obtain. Restaurants are good sources if you don't want to buy five gallons of wine or champagne just to get the empties. It is best to use only those bottles that are tinted. While exposure to light is not nearly as great a problem with wine as it is with beer, some wine is slightly affected by light. All champagne bottles are tinted. Many screw-top wine bottles are not. If you are unable to find tinted bottles, use the clear glass variety, but store them in a dark place. You will need a quart-size bottle for the decanting procedure. The ideal type is the screw-top beer bottle.

To facilitate storage, go to the liquor store and ask for two shipping cartons for wine bottles. These are cardboard boxes which have separate divisions for twelve bottles and which can be stacked on top of each other to minimize the space required for storage. If you use champagne bottles, you will need the larger champagne shipping cartons.

MISCELLANEOUS ITEMS

You will need the following everyday items which you probably already have around the house: a large saucepan; a long-handled plastic spoon; a measuring cup; a large roll of Scotch or masking tape; extra-wide Saran Wrap. The extra-wide wrap is often hard to find. A highly satisfactory substitute is the disposable plastic wrapping which laundries and cleaners place over clothes. You will also need a long-handled bottle brush. This item is included in the standard fermentation kit.

CLEANING

It is very important to keep all your wine-making equipment and bottles absolutely clean. Do not use soap or other detergents as they will leave a microscopic film on the equipment which tends to impart a taste to the wine. Use only hot water to clean your equipment. This must be done as soon as possible after it is used because the wine and yeast deposits are much harder to clean off if they are given a chance to dry. Use a small hand brush to clean the inside of the primary fermenter and flush out the carboy with hot water after use. Use a hand spray if there is one attached to your kitchen sink. This should be repeated several times to ensure that all the yeast particles have been dislodged. The siphon hose must be rinsed through with hot water immediately after use. The carboy should be stored without the cap on so that air can circulate freely into it. Just before using the two vessels and the siphon hose for the next batch of wine, rinse them out thoroughly once more to remove dust and other particles.

Prior to making the first batch, the unused primary and secondary fermenters must be "cured" to remove the slight industrial film common to all new polyethylene. To do this, fill the secondary fermenter halfway with warm water. Next, add a one-pound box of ordinary baking or washing soda. Screw the cap on and swill the solution around several times; then let it sit on its side for several hours. Turn it to the other side for several more hours. This will dissolve the industrial film entirely. Pour the solution into the primary fermenter, and rinse out the secondary fermenter several times with a spray of hot water to remove all traces of the baking soda. The primary fermenter can be cured much quicker since there is room to reach inside. Simply pour in the warm water and baking soda and scrub the inside vigorously with paper towels; then rinse it out. It is a good idea to give the vessels a quick rinse with a normal strength baking soda solution after every other batch to keep them fresh.

When first acquiring bottles, clean them out with a hot water spray and the bottle brush if there is dried wine inside. They should then be put through the dishwasher without detergent to sterilize them, especially if they have been used before. They should be turned neck down to dry and stored the same way when empty to prevent dust from entering. They will not need cleaning with a bottle brush, nor will they need sterilizing again after you use them, providing you spray them out with hot water immediately after emptying the wine from the bottle and turn them upside down to dry. You will only need to spray each bottle once prior to using it again to ensure total cleanliness. The plastic corks or screw tops should also be rinsed clean after use.

Tape

Saran Wrap

FIGURE 1

Primary fermenter

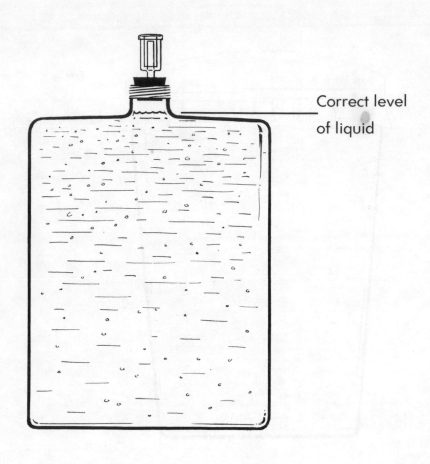

Correct level
of liquid

FIGURE 2

Secondary fermenter (carboy) with fermentation lock attached

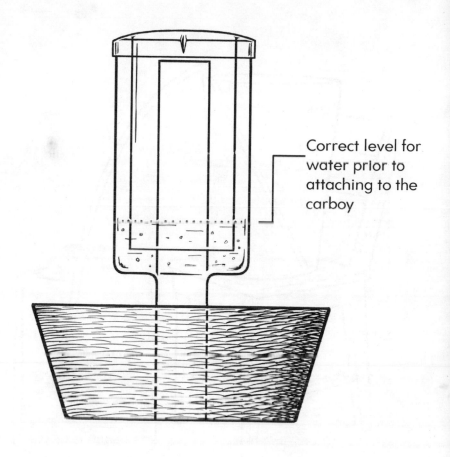

Correct level for water prior to attaching to the carboy

FIGURE 3

Fermentation lock

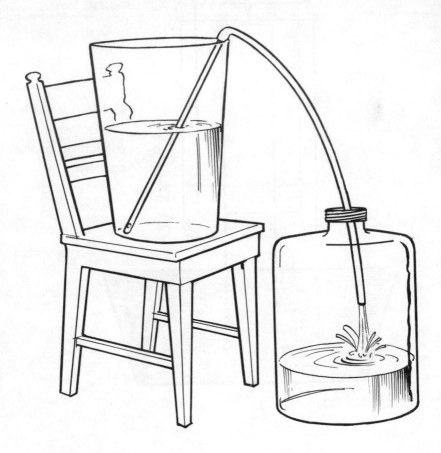

FIGURE 4

Siphoning. To start the flow of beer or wine, suck on the lower end as you would on a straw until the flow is established. The flow end must be kept lower than the drawing end for the flow to continue

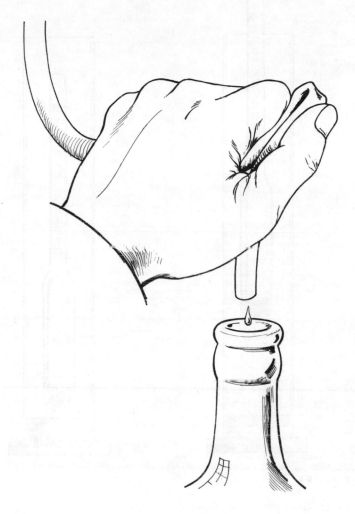

FIGURE 5

Example of how to cut off the flow of siphoning tube to avoid spillage when bottling

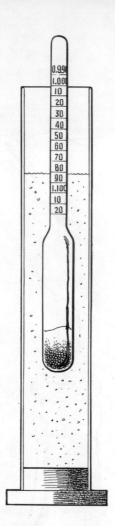

FIGURE 6

Left: *Example of hydrometer reading of 1.082, the average specific gravity of the wine mix prior to fermentation*

Right: *Hydrometer reading of 0.995, the average specific gravity reading for most of the wines in this book after fermentation is finished*

Ingredients

GRAPE CONCENTRATE

As I mentioned in the beginning of this book, it is no longer necessary to acquire raw grapes or to plant a vineyard to be able to produce a superb wine at home. Several of the major wineries in this country are now producing grape concentrate formulated specifically for the home wine maker. The pure wine concentrate is made from the juice of the *vinifera* grape. The pulp and seeds have been removed so that the initial steps of crushing and straining, a messy and tedious procedure, have already been accomplished. The brand of concentrate which we will deal with is called Bear Mountain. This is not to say that there are not other fine brands available, but the Bear Mountain, California, winery is very large, and their product is obtainable from most wine supply outlets throughout the

United States. There are several flavors of concentrate available in quart and gallon sizes. These are:

CONCENTRATE	TYPE
Red	(Burgundy)
White	(Chablis)
Pink	(vin rosé)
Cold Duck	(blend of various grapes)
Muscat	(Muscatel)
Ruby Cabernet	(Claret)
Semillon	(dry white wine)
French Colombard	(a hearty wine sometimes used in champagnes)

People invariably ask which concentrate flavors are best. While this is strictly a matter of individual taste, my preference is for the standard red grape concentrate or, for white wines, either the white or semillon. These three flavor types are much more mellow than the varietals or the other blends. Since they also come in quart sizes, you can easily blend them to produce rosés or any degree of flavor you desire, and they will still maintain their mellowness. For a rosé, for example, instead of using one gallon of concentrate, use three quarts of white and one of red.

None of these concentrates has any sediment, and since the fermentation method detailed in this book completes the fermentation in a relatively short time, the wine requires no racking. There is one important point to remember when using the Bear Mountain concentrates, however. They are sterilized at the winery with sulphur dioxide. For this reason, it is not necessary to use bisulphite tablets to sterilize the wine when it is mixed at home. In fact, the tablets must not be used, or the sulphur dioxide level will be raised to the point where even the pure yeast culture may be killed. You may find that some of the concentrates have instructions for using the bisulphite tablets, these tablets may even be included in the package; nonetheless, they must not be used. Other brands of concentrate may need to have bisulphite tablets added to sterilize them if this has not been done at the winery. Generally, if the concentrate comes in cans, it will need bisulphiting. The sterilizing agent does not last in metal containers and is therefore not added at the wineries. Bear Mountain concentrates are packed in plastic containers to prevent the sulphur dioxide from being degraded. For concentrates which need bisulphite, use two 4-gram tablets per gallon of wine after the water is added, or ten tablets for a five-gallon batch. The tablets must be thoroughly crushed into solution in a cup of warm water prior to stirring into the wine. The wine mix should then sit overnight before adding the yeast.

The recipes in this book call for the use of one gallon of concentrate, the amount required to make up a five-gallon batch of wine. The cost of the concentrate in one gallon containers is generally under ten dollars, including shipping.

YEAST

It is very important to use only true wine yeast for your fermentation. There are many brands available through wine makers' supply firms, some satisfactory for home wine making and some not. In my opinion, the best yeast available for the home wine maker is Montrachet Active Dry Yeast. It is put out by Universal Foods Corporation in 5-gram foil packs. This yeast is also used by many of the commercial wineries in this country, and a pack is included in one-gallon shipments of Bear Mountain and other concentrates. This yeast was developed several years ago in the wine laboratories of the University of California at Davis and is referred to at Universal Foods as Strain 522 UCLA-Davis. The yeast has a high tolerance for sulphur dioxide, maintains a vigorous and rapid fermentation, and starts soon after being added to the mix. It is very important in wine making to have a fast-starting yeast; if the mix remains dormant for much longer than a day, the chance of spoilage increases due to airborne molds and bacteria. The Montrachet yeast will usually form a head within twenty-four hours after being added to the mix. Accompanying the head will be a protective layer of carbon dioxide gas to shield the wine. I do not recommend using any of the liquid yeast cultures that are on the market. They are slow and usually require a few days in a starter solution to begin active fermentation. This is a needless waste of time, and sometimes the starter solution spoils during the lengthy dormant period. These cultures also cost much more than the recommended type. Some people try to economize in their wine making by reclaiming some of their yeast from the fermenter and using it for the next batch, but this should never be done. Since the Montrachet comes free with the concentrates, there can be no possible saving, and the chance of spoilage is greatly increased due to the difficulty in maintaining a sterile environment for the yeast between batches. The Montrachet in its unopened pack will last almost indefinitely, as it is dry and vacuum-packed under nitrogen.

NUTRIENT

A chemical which is added to the mix at the same time as the yeast. The yeast cells require a healthy environment in which to carry on a vigorous reproduction. Without the addition of yeast nutrient, the fermentation would become very sluggish or cease altogether. This phenomenon is referred to, appropriately enough, as a stuck ferment. When this happens, it is very hard to get the process going again. The nutrient is a trace element; only four level teaspoons are needed for a five-gallon batch. This will ensure rapid fermentation with no chance of a stuck ferment or even a sluggish one.

ACID BLEND

Used to give the wine its characteristic slightly tart flavor. Without this ingredient, wine would have an insipid taste. By raising the acid level of the mix, the acid blend also acts as a preventative against spoilage organisms. It is an inexpensive combination of simple fruit acids, usually citric, malic, and tartaric acids in equal amounts, available through any wine makers' supply firm. For the recipes in this book, only one ounce or less of acid blend is required for a five-gallon batch of wine.

FINING POWDER

Used to render the wine clear and brilliant. Only one half level teaspoon is needed for a five-gallon batch. The finings combine with the tannin present in the mix to form a colloid solution which carries any suspended sediment to the bottom of the secondary fermenter. For the finings to be effective, they must be approximately equal in weight to the amount of tannin in the wine. If more than one half level teaspoon is used, the finings themselves could remain in suspension and cause a slight haze in the wine. If no finings are used, the wine could have a slight tannin haze, along with other suspended matter.

ASCORBIC ACID

Pure vitamin C, used in home wine making to prevent oxidation of the wine. It is added to the wine just before bottling and, as with the fining powder, only one half level teaspoon is needed. This will ensure uniformly high-quality wine by effectively preventing any oxidation of the wine while it is aging in bottles or during the decanting procedure prior to drinking it. There is also a fringe benefit to this addition of vitamin C. One half teaspoon equals 2,500 milligrams. Divided by twenty-five bottles, that amounts to one hundred milligrams per bottle. Since the minimum daily requirement of vitamin C has been established at thirty milligrams, each bottle of wine contains over 300 percent of your daily requirement. This holds true since very little of the ascorbic acid is itself oxidized after being added to the wine. Please don't misconstrue this observation on the healthful aspects of wine. I'm certainly not recommending that you make a wholesale substitution of a bottle of wine in place of your morning orange juice. The vitamin C would give you a healthy glow, most assuredly, but this benefit would be more than offset by the look of condemnation you would receive from your associates as you stumbled into work later.

SUGAR

Used in wine making for two purposes: to provide enough sugar during the fermentation stage to give the wine its optimum alcohol content and to sweeten the wine to taste during the decanting procedure if other than a dry wine is desired. A notable difference between this book and other wine books currently on the market, especially those from England and Canada, is that our procedure will turn out a very palatable wine in just nine weeks from the time the ingredients are mixed. Other books use a process which requires almost a year from the time of mixing to the time the wine can be consumed. The sugar content of the wine plays a major part in the last fermentation process used in this book. We will add just enough sugar to the mix to bring the specific gravity reading to between 1.080 and 1.085. As mentioned earlier, this will give the wine an alcohol content of approximately 12 percent, the same as most of the finest French wines. To accomplish this, sugar is added to the mix. You can use either ordinary granulated household sugar or corn sugar, also known as dextrose; both are entirely satisfactory. Some wine makers claim that the use of corn sugar will result in a slightly smoother wine, and this is certainly true in recipes calling for large amounts of sugar. The yeast converts the sugar into alcohol and carbon dioxide gas during fermentation; with household sugar, when the sweetness is gone, only the taste of the cane is left, and this tends to be sharp and cidery. Since the amount of sugar used in these recipes is relatively small, however, the difference in taste is undetectable. If you do decide to use corn sugar, however, it is generally available through two sources: your friendly neighborhood drugstore will sell it for five to ten dollars for four pounds, or you can get the same amount through any wine makers' supply firm for about one dollar! Do not use corn syrups from the grocery store as a substitute or your batch of wine will be a disaster—they have milk products and vanilla in them.

WATER

It is essential to use good water when making wine. The vast majority of water systems in this country provide water of sufficiently high quality. In Europe this is not the case, and so most books on wine making, especially those that originated overseas or in Canada, call for boiling or otherwise sterilizing the water. This is not a necessary procedure in this country because the purity of our water is well within the limits required for making wine.

However, there are some areas where the taste of the water might affect the taste of the wine. Fortunately, this problem is easily remedied. If you think your drinking water has too strong a sulphur taste, you can take your carboy to a firm that supplies water to office water machines and have them fill it up at a nominal fee. If your water system has an excessive amount of minerals in it, such as iron, you can purchase a small tap filter from a health food store for under five dollars. These are usually polymer ion filters, and they effectively remove over 90 percent of the iron and some other minerals from the water as it passes through. If your water supply has a pronounced chlorine taste to it but is otherwise normal, there is no problem at all—the chlorine will dissipate completely from the wine mix after the first day of active fermentation, leaving no taste. Try not to be overly concerned if your water system has only a slight off-taste to it, as this will not ordinarily affect the wine at all. It is only in cases where the water has a pronounced off-flavor that you would need to use the above remedies. Do not make the mistake of using distilled water for any fermented beverage. This water is flat and will impart an insipid character to whatever you are making.

The Fast Fermentation Process

I mentioned earlier that the main recipes in this book use a fast fermentation process which will turn out a good wine in about nine weeks, as opposed to the ten to twelve months required using the older methods. An explanation of both methods will give you an appreciation of the advantages of the newer process.

Traditionally, home wine makers, along with home brewers, have striven to produce a beverage with as much alcohol content as possible. Some have done this under the mistaken notion that for their wine to be as good as or better than commercial brands, it had to have a greater "kick" to it. Others were simply following recipes from wine books which called for a great amount of sugar in the mix. Indeed, most books on the subject of home wine making list a procedure which turns out wines with an alcohol content of 14 percent or higher. Not that there is anything wrong with wines having a high alcohol content. Ports and sherries, for instance, generally average 19 to 20 percent alcohol, and they certainly couldn't retain their character as dessert wines without this much. Dinner wines, on the other hand, vary considerably in alcohol content, ranging from about 10 to 14 percent. The quality of a wine is in no way determined by its alcohol content. If you will examine various bottles of domestic and imported wines in your local store, you will see that some wines with 14 percent alcohol will cost one or two dollars a bottle. Other wines with alcohol contents of only 10 or 11 percent may cost seven to ten dollars, and considerably more for vintage years. Most of the finest French wines average 12 percent alcohol.

The regular wines in this book will also have an alcohol content of 12 percent. By setting this as the optimum, the fermentation and aging period is reduced from the ten to twelve months required in the old methods to a total of nine weeks. To understand how this more efficient fermentation takes place, it is necessary to see how yeast performs its function in the fermentation process. In the sugary environment of the grape mix, the yeast multiplies by cell division. During this reproductive cycle, the yeast feeds on the sugars and converts them to alcohol and to carbon dioxide gas. As fermentation continues and the alcohol content increases, the yeast begins to slow down in its cycle of reproduction. This is because yeast can tolerate only a certain amount of its own by-product, alcohol.

In wine mix which has enough sugar to give a final alcohol content of 14 percent, the yeast will carry on a vigorous ferment for the first 12 or 13 percent and then slow down drastically as the alcohol content approaches 14 percent. This is the normal limit of alcohol that the yeast can tolerate before it is killed or becomes dormant.* It requires months for the yeast to convert the sugars to achieve those last two percentage points of alcohol. During this period, the wine must be racked to prevent it from resting too long on the yeast layer, which will produce off-flavors. Because of these rackings (generally racked every three months) and the excessive time the wine remains in the carboys, some oxidation often develops. This can give the wine a bitter taste and discolor it. These problems will not arise using the fast fermentation method. By using only enough sugar to produce 12 percent alcohol, the yeast carries on its vigorous reproductive cycle throughout the fermentation. Since it is not affected greatly by the 12 percent alcohol in the wine, it consumes the sugar completely in a relatively brief period of time and has a short, slow fermentation at the end simply because there is only a slight amount of sugar remaining to be converted. Normally, the wine ferments in the primary fermenter for six days, is transferred to the secondary fermenter for one month, is aged in bottles one month, and then is decanted, ready to serve.

The relative quality of wines made with the fast fermentation method is superior to that produced by the older method. Aside from the elimination of the oxidation hazard and the shorter period that the wine rests on the yeast layer, the flavor is much richer and the bouquet

* The Montrachet dry yeast can actually tolerate about 16 percent before becoming dormant, although it, too, slows down prior to reaching this level of alcohol.

much more pronounced. Under the older methods, much of the delicate flavor and aroma are dissipated through the fermentation lock during the extensive aging period, whereas ours are preserved intact in bottles after the rapid fermentation. In addition, the steps involved in making the wine are much simpler, since racking has been eliminated, along with the expense of having to buy extra carboys.

Procedure for Wine

The following chapter gives a detailed step-by-step procedure for making wine. This includes everything you will need to know: from the mixing of the ingredients to the decanting and serving of the finished wine. To simplify the measuring of the exact amount of water required in the recipes, the secondary fermenter is used as a guide. This is part of the same kit mentioned on page 110. For those who already have equipment, the actual amount of water is specified by volume. Until recently, lack of availability of correct equipment and ingredients was a major problem for the home wine maker, but this difficulty has disappeared with the development of a standardized unit. The kit contains all the needed equipment and the correct yeasts and additives. All you will need to obtain will be the particular flavor of grape concentrate you desire. Order forms for this are in these kits, which include a list from a wine makers' supply firm. For measuring purposes, the five-gallon secondary fermenter has an actual capacity of 5½ gallons.

Once you have read the detailed section, a procedure outline is included at the end of each wine section as an easy-to-follow reference while you are actually making the wine.

INGREDIENTS FOR FIVE GALLONS OF WINE

1 *gallon Bear Mountain grape concentrate*
4½ *gallons water*
8 *measuring cups sugar (4 pounds)*
4 *level teaspoons acid blend*
4 *level teaspoons nutrient*
1 *pack Montrachet active dry yeast*
½ *level teaspoon finings*
½ *level teaspoon ascorbic acid*
Initial specific gravity 1.080–1.085
Final specific gravity .990–.995

NOTE: For a heavy-bodied wine, use 1 gallon plus 1 quart of concentrate instead of one gallon, and use only one pound of sugar.

After you have thoroughly cured your primary and secondary fermenters using the method detailed on page 35, fill the secondary fermenter with cold water to a point three inches from the top. Transfer enough of this water to a large saucepan to fill it halfway. Add four pounds of sugar to the saucepan and, stirring, heat it on the stove sufficiently to allow the sugar to dissolve completely into solution. Next, transfer all except about a quart of the remaining water in the secondary fermenter to the primary fermenter. The secondary fermenter is used merely as our water measure at this stage. The mixing and the initial fermentation take place in the primary fermenter. Pour the saucepanful of sugar solution into the primary fermenter. Add four level teaspoons each of acid blend and nutrient to the solution in the primary fermenter. The next step is the addition of the grape concentrate. Prior to opening the plastic container of concentrate, it is a good idea to rinse off the area around the opening with the hand spray on the kitchen sink. This effectively cleans off any juice that might have spilled over during filling at the winery and washes away any wild yeasts that may have thus formed. Before unscrewing the cap, pull the whole piece out, as this is a pouring spout. Pour the concentrate into the primary fermenter; then add the small amount of water left in the secondary fermenter to the concentrate container and replace the cap. Shake vigorously to dislodge all the grape sediment adhering to the bottom of the container, and pour this into the primary fermenter. It is very important to retain all of this residue for the wine mix as these are some of the grape acids which have settled out during storage. These add significantly to a healthy fermentation, and they also add to the character and bouquet of the finished wine. Stir the wine mix with a long-handled spoon to ensure that the additives are dissolved into solution. The specific gravity at this point will read between 1.080 and 1.085. The reason for the slight variation in initial gravity from batch to batch is due to normal variations in the grape sugar content of the concentrate.

The next step is the addition of the Montrachet yeast. Prior to adding the yeast to the mix, reactivate it by pouring it into a cup of warm water. Some of the Montrachet comes in envelopes which suggest simply pouring the dry yeast directly into the wine mix, but this is not desirable. Sometimes the dry granules will remain on the surface and form a top fermentation, instead of settling to the bottom where they belong, causing a messy situation with a thick layer of yeast floating on top of the wine mix. Universal Foods Corporation, makers of the Montrachet yeast, recommends that it be reconstituted in water at a temperature between 105° and 110° F.; if you want to be a perfectionist, you can adjust the temperature to this range with a small medical thermometer, but in actual practice I have found that the yeast reconstitutes just as rapidly and completely in warm water of various temperatures. Just be sure that the water is not actually hot. The yeast cells are killed when the temperature exceeds 115°. When you pour the dry yeast into a cup of the warm water, it first settles to the bottom. Within ten minutes, however, it swells up and rises to the top. When it has all risen to form a creamy head on the surface of the water in the cup, stir it moderately until it goes into solution. Make sure that all the yeast lumps are completely dissolved; then pour the cup of yeast water into the primary fermenter. Mix it in thoroughly by stirring with a spoon. Using this method you will never have a problem with any yeast forming on the top of the wine mix. There is another advantage to mixing the yeast in warm water rather than adding it directly when dry. A much greater percentage of the yeast cells will reactivate, and the fermentation will get off to a faster start.

After the yeast has been added, cover the primary fermenter with Saran Wrap or plastic clothes-covering material from the cleaners. Seal it with tape as shown in Figure 1, although not too tightly. Cover the top of the primary fermenter with a piece of cloth to keep out the light, although this can be removed to inspect the mix from time to time without affecting the wine in any way. The entire fermentation should be carried out at normal room temperatures, between 65° and 75°. You will notice that within ten to twenty hours after adding the yeast, a foamy head will form on the surface of the mix. This indicates the beginning of the primary, or tumultuous, fermentation. It is a good idea to have several sheets of newspaper underneath the primary fermenter. The vigorous fermentation on some occasions causes large bubbles to form which swell to the height of the covering and pop, allowing a small amount of the juice to run down the side of the fermenter. Before you start to visualize a flood of wine over your floor, let me assure you that this seepage, if it happens at all, will be very slight. It will not exceed one or two spoonfuls. You may ask, "Why not use a primary fermenter with a capacity of greater than seven gallons to eliminate the problem entirely?" The answer is that the space in the fermenter should be large enough to allow the foamy head to rise, but not so large that there is an excessive amount of air space between the wine and the cover. This is to prevent any chance of oxidation from excessive contact with the air prior to the onset of fermentation, and later when the primary fermentation slows down. The seven-gallon capacity is the ideal compromise. Again, however, the slight overflow rarely occurs.

Billowing is caused by the formation of carbon dioxide gas, which bubbles out of the fermenting wine. Since the gas is heavier than air, all air is expelled from the fermenter and a protective layer of carbon dioxide rests on the surface to shield the wine. During the first two or three days of active fermentation, the plastic covering retains foam from the large bubbles. After these initial bubbles subside, you can replace the plastic sheet with a clean piece, wiping off the top rim of the vessel at the same time. As with the first sheet of plastic, do not tape it so tightly that the gas cannot escape with just a moderate billowing.

The primary fermentation will ordinarily take six days to complete, although it could take up to nine days, depending on the temperature. The hydrometer is used to tell when the primary fermentation is over. On the sixth day after adding the yeast, check the specific gravity by removing the cover and inserting the hydrometer. Clear the surface foam away from the area of the stem so that you can get an accurate reading. If it reads 1.000 or lower, it is time to transfer the wine to the secondary fermenter. In some instances, especially with lighter wines, the gravity after just six or seven days in the primary fermenter may go down to around .990. This is quite normal and only indicates a very efficient fermentation. If the specific gravity is appreciably higher than 1.000, for instance, 1.005, replace the cover and let the wine work out another day or two; then take another reading.

Give the secondary fermenter a quick rinse to remove any dust particles which may have accumulated in it over the week. Next, prepare the fining solution which is added during siphoning. Sprinkle a one-half level teaspoon of fining powder into a small saucepan containing approximately one cup of warm water. Let it sit for ten minutes to allow time for some of the finings to dissolve; then bring the solution to just below boiling temperature on the stove, stirring all the while with a small spoon. When you see that all the fining granules are dissolved, remove the saucepan from the heat.

It is now time to siphon the wine from the primary to the secondary fermenter. For those of you who have never siphoned before, it is necessary to have the primary fermenter at a greater height than the secondary fermenter. For ideal siphoning speed, both for transferring and later for bottling, the primary fermenter should be on a stand or chair about twenty-one inches off the floor. Place the drawing end of the siphon unit halfway into the wine in the primary fermenter. Hold the flow end lower than the drawing end and suck evenly until the flow is established. It is best to have a pan close by so that you don't spill any on the floor. Pinch off the flow as shown in Figure 5, then place the flow end into the secondary fermenter. If you are using the standard home fermentation kit, the drawing end of the siphon hose can be lowered at this point to the bottom of the primary fermenter; the hole openings are above the yeast layer height. With other types of siphons, you will have to judge the yeast layer and hold the siphon above it to keep from sucking up too much of the yeast into the secondary fermenter. About halfway through the siphoning, pour the fining solution into the secondary fermenter. Do this very carefully so as not to spill any of the rather sticky solution on the sides of the fermenter or on the siphon hose. It should not be necessary to interrupt the siphoning to do this. Let the flow continue until the wine is completely transferred to the secondary fermenter. The reason for adding the fining solution during the siphoning is to ensure an even distribution throughout the wine.

Place the secondary fermenter on a stand or chair where it can remain undisturbed for one month. If the wine did not quite fill up the secondary fermenter, add water to bring the level up to just below the neck. It is important to have very little air space in the carboy during this secondary fermentation. Fill the fermentation lock to a depth of only one-half inch water and attach it to the carboy. You will soon notice that the lock will bubble. This is the carbon dioxide gas escaping. The lock prevents any air from entering the carboy because the water effectively seals out the air while allowing gas to escape.

The secondary fermentation, as with the primary fermentation, is carried out at normal room temperature, ideally 70°. Place a towel around the secondary fermenter to keep out light. During the month of aging in the secondary fermenter, do not take off the lock to see how things are going. This defeats the purpose of the anaerobic fermentation. Bubbling of the lock will in most cases be so slow as to be unnoticeable, but this is quite normal. During this period, the residual sugars are fermented into alcohol and carbon dioxide gas by the yeast. The final specific gravity of the wine at the end of one month in the secondary fermenter will be .990 to .995, less than the weight of water due to the alcohol content. Also during this period, the yeast settles to a firm layer on the bottom and the wine becomes partially clear.

After thirty days in the secondary fermenter, the wine is siphoned carefully off the yeast layer into the primary fermenter. Before doing this, rinse out the primary fermenter with hot water. Add one half level teaspoon of ascorbic acid to the primary fermenter before siphoning the wine into it. This small amount of ascorbic acid will prevent any oxidation from taking place in the wine, either during the siphoning, or later on after the decanting procedure.

The next step is an important one in that it aids greatly in mellowing the wine. With the wine in the primary fermenter, take a long-handled spoon and stir vigorously back and forth. This will cause moderate foaming at the surface. The purpose of this procedure is to dissipate the gases from the wine which, if left in, would give it a harsh flavor. These are called malo-lactic gases and are formed as the wine goes through its process of mellowing, or malo-lactic fermentation. These gases are very small in quantity compared to the large amount of carbon dioxide gas formed during the primary and secondary fermentation; yet they are very harsh-tasting and must be dissipated before the wine can become mellow. The wine should be agitated in the primary fermenter for several minutes until there is no more foaming on the surface. When this is accomplished, the wine can be siphoned into bottles.

The bottles should be filled to the same height as commercial wine bottles. If using screw-top bottles, cap the bottles loosely for the first day to allow the wine to breathe out residual gases. If you use champagne bottles with plastic stoppers, just place these upside down on the opening of the bottles the first day to keep dust particles out of the wine. Next day, tighten the screw tops or push in the stoppers. The plastic stoppers must be soaked in hot water prior to inserting them, or it will be most difficult to force them into the necks. Do not dry them after removing them from the water, as the wetness also helps in the insertion. Just give them each a flick of the wrist to remove excess water.

The wine should be aged upright in the bottles at room temperature for thirty days. During this period, the remaining trace of yeast from the secondary fermentation will settle to a film on the bottom of the bottles, and the wine will become brilliant. This can be observed after the second week of aging by holding up a bottle to the light and seeing the sharp image of the light passing through the clear wine. This process continues until about the fourth week of aging. At the same time, the malo-lactic fermentation continues its process of mellowing, resulting in the formation of more malo-lactic gases in the wine.

The final step in the wine-making procedure prior to drinking is to decant the wine and shake it to dissipate the remaining malo-lactic gases. This should be done bottle by bottle as the wine is consumed. To decant, simply pour slowly from the fifth-size aging bottle to a quart-size decanting bottle. Quart-size beer bottles with screw tops are the most practical. Try not to bubble the wine too much at the neck when pouring. The idea is to decant as much of the clear wine as possible off the slight yeast film on the bottom of the bottle. This is accomplished by pouring steadily without interrupting the flow. You will be able to pour all but the last half inch or so of wine from the bottle in this manner. When finished, screw the top on the quart bottle containing the decanted wine and shake it vigorously. Loosen the top to release the malo-lactic gases. You will easily be able to hear the gas escaping under pressure as you do this. Tighten the top and repeat the shaking process several times until no more gas is apparently being released. Ordinarily, this will require seven such shakings. The wine should then be put in the refrigerator overnight with the top on loosely so that the residual gases can escape and complete the mellowing process. Be sure to rinse out the aging bottle with the hand spray to dislodge the yeast film on the bottom; then place it upside down to drain dry. This way it will not have to be sterilized or scrubbed out again with the bottle brush—it will require only a quick rinse with hot water prior to its next use.

After the wine has been allowed to breathe for twenty-four hours, it is ready to drink. If it is not all finished at one time, it can be kept for many days in the refrigerator. After the first twenty-four hours it can be capped tightly. The ascorbic acid in the wine will prevent oxidation even if the bottle is more than half empty. The importance of agitation of the wine prior to bottling and again after decanting cannot be overemphasized. The malo-lactic gases must be removed before the wine can achieve its superb character and mellowness.

Our wine-making procedure will always turn out a dry wine. If you prefer a sweeter wine, simply follow this procedure. After decanting the wine, and prior to shaking it, mix up a sugar solution by heating up two parts sugar to one part water in a saucepan. When the sugar is completely dissolved into solution, pour one half ounce or three level teaspoons of the sugar syrup into the wine. This amount of sugar solution will produce a pleasingly mellow wine. If a sweeter wine is desired, increase the amount of sugar solution accordingly. Don't overdo it though: a little sweetener goes a long way! This method of sweetening wine is far superior to the old method whereby a greater amount of sugar was initially added to the wine mix than could be fermented out. This necessitated the long-drawn-out fermentation, which is not desirable, and the result would be twenty-five bottles of wine with exactly the same sweetness. With our sweetening procedure, there is an infinite choice of wine, from dry to very sweet, so that each bottle can be prepared exactly as desired to suit the occasion.

While the fast fermentation process will produce a very palatable wine after just one month of aging in the bottle, the wine mellows considerably and becomes even better after three months of aging. After six months of bottle aging, it can be classified as excellent and fully matured. Thereafter, it maintains a peak flavor for a year or more, depending on the type of wine. Red wines generally maintain a peak for a much longer period of time than do white wines; however the whites mellow and mature faster than do the reds.

SERVING YOUR WINES

These wines should always be chilled before serving. In Europe many wines are served at room temperature, but this is not the general custom in most sections of this country. Homes are traditionally kept much cooler overseas than in the United States, where our average room temperature is around 70°. This is much too warm for serving any wine. Some delicate wines are diminished in flavor by chilling but this is not so with these home-made wines. The robust, full-bodied flavors are enhanced by chilling— within reason. As for the type of glass to use for these wines, most people prefer clear glass goblets. These glasses allow you to enjoy not only the taste of the wine but also to see its clarity and color. Because of the fullness of the goblet, which tapers slightly toward the opening, like a tulip, the bouquet of the wine is concentrated at the top. The glass should be filled only slightly over halfway. This allows for a richer bouquet to develop. The only problem is that most "standard" wineglasses in this country are about half as large as they should be, and they don't allow for a very generous serving of wine between pourings. Some astute shopping for full-size glasses should solve this problem, however.

There are several wine servers or decanters on the market which add a festive touch to the serving of your wines when you have guests. One such server contains a plastic ice filler inserted into the top to keep the wine cool. This is not desirable because the acetate plastic filler affects the flavor of the wine. My preference for wine servers is the green-tinted glass server with the curved spout imported from Italy. This server has a hollow bulb blown into the side into which ice can be put to keep the wine cool throughout dinner. You can find them at glassware stores and wine makers' supply outlets, usually for less than ten dollars. The wine can simply be transferred to these servers after it has been shaken in the quart bottle and left overnight in the refrigerator to breathe. These servers hold about two bottles of wine—the most practical amount if you're serving four people or more. Remember, your wines will keep much longer than the store-bought variety if you have some left over, due to the added ascorbic acid.

Now that you have read this detailed procedure, use the following outline as an easy reference during your actual wine-making operation.

PROCEDURE OUTLINE

INGREDIENTS

1 gallon Bear Mountain concentrate
4½ U.S. gallons of water
8 level cups sugar (4 pounds)
4 level teaspoons acid blend
4 level teaspoons nutrient
Montrachet active dry wine yeast
½ level teaspoon fining powder
½ level teaspoon ascorbic acid

EQUIPMENT

Rigid primary fermenter— 7 gallons
Rigid secondary fermenter— 5½ gallons
Large saucepan
Hydrometer
Extra-wide plastic sheet
Masking or Scotch tape
Measuring cup
Siphon unit
25 fifth-size bottles, tops
1-quart bottle

NOTE: For a heavy-bodied wine use 1 gallon plus 1 quart of concentrate and only 1 pound of sugar.

1. Fill carboy to 3 inches from top with cold water. Pour some of that water into large saucepan and heat. Pour in 4 pounds of sugar and dissolve.

2. Add 4 level teaspoons each acid blend and nutrient to primary fermenter. Transfer all but 1 quart of water from carboy to primary fermenter. Pour in sugar water from saucepan. Add concentrate, rinse its container thoroughly with remaining water from carboy, and add to mix.

3. Pour pack of yeast into cup of warm water (105°–110°). After 10 minutes, stir completely, pour directly into wine mix, stir. Cover primary fermenter with plastic sheet, seal with tape. Cover with cloth. Allow to ferment until specific gravity reaches 1.000 or lower, usually 6 days.

4. Siphon wine into carboy. Dissolve finings solution in warm water and add during siphoning. Top up carboy with water to just below neck, if needed. Attach fermentation lock filled ½ inch with water. Wrap cloth around carboy to keep out light. Age 30 days.

5. Siphon wine carefully off yeast layer into primary fermenter containing ½ level teaspoon ascorbic acid. Agitate wine by stirring vigorously with long spoon until malo-lactic gases dissipate.

6. Siphon into bottles, cap loosely for one day, then tighten caps. Store upright at room temperature for 30 days.

7. Decant into quart bottle, leaving slight yeast film behind. If sweet wine is desired, add 3 level teaspoons sugar syrup to the bottle. Shake vigorously several times, each time releasing malo-lactic gases from the bottle. Store in refrigerator overnight with cap loose to allow all residual gases to dissipate from the wine. Serve chilled.

Sherry

Sherry is a heavy dessert or cocktail wine characterized by a pleasing nutlike flavor. The name is derived from the Spanish town of Jerez. Jerez de la Frontera has been in existence for over three thousand years and is the source of the world's finest sherries. Unlike other wines, there can be no vintage year for sherry because all sherries are a blend of several years of selected wines. This is accomplished in Jerez by the famous Solera system, in which aging barrels of wine are stacked above each other, the oldest on the bottom. These barrels are connected to each other so that the youngest sherry, on the top layer of barrels, flows down into lower barrels and blends with more mature sherry. This process is accomplished by bottling only from the lowest, or oldest, barrels. As a void is created in these barrels, it is filled up with sherry from the next higher barrel, and so on up the line. Practically speaking, sherry blends with other sherries from seven to ten years old, as the Soleras are normally stacked seven to ten high. Looking at it another way, though, the blend can have some sherry in it that may be hundreds of years old, depending on when the first layer of barrels was laid down. Since the bottom barrels (and all others) are being replenished simultaneously as they are emptied, a certain amount of the very first blend is always, theoretically at least, in the barrel, and a certain amount will end up being bottled. Naturally the original blends are constantly being diluted, and over the ages the amount of remaining early sherries pales into insignificance, but it is still an interesting thing to ponder as you savor your next glass of Spanish sherry.

The richness of sherry is enhanced by the addition of syrups comprised of raisin extracts, and long aging in oak barrels imparts a nutlike flavor to the wine. Some California wineries bake the wine in barrels for several months at a temperature of between 100° and 140° to make the flavor even more pronounced. The unique taste of the true Spanish sherries, however, is achieved by a method of fermentation quite different from the baking process. Unlike the anaerobic method of fermentation used for most wines, true sherry is made partially by an *aerobic* fermentation. This allows a type of airborne yeast, called a flor, to settle on the wine and form a yeast bloom on the surface. This flor formation does not take place until the initial tumultuous fermentation with regular wine yeast has ended. When the flor finally forms in the aerobic environment at the surface of the wine, it causes a certain oxidation and leads to the formation of the esters which give sherry its characteristic flavor. The flor continues its buildup on the surface; when the desired amount of flavor is achieved, the wine is run off into another container, and brandy is added to bring the alcohol content to the desired level and to stop the fermentation. With the addition of brandy, the alcohol content of most Spanish sherries is brought to between 16 and 19 percent, depending on the particular sherry being produced. It is possible to make an excellent Spanish type of sherry in the home. Universal Foods Corporation, the firm that makes the Montrachet yeast, also makes a flor-sherry yeast which forms the all-important bloom on top of the wine. Following is the procedure for making either a deep red oloroso or a light fino sherry.

PROCEDURE

Fill secondary fermenter to a height of five inches from the top for the initial water measure. This amounts to 3¾ gallons. Pour some of this water into a large saucepan, heat, and dissolve two pounds of sugar into solution. Next, transfer all except a small amount of the remaining water in the secondary fermenter to the primary fermenter. The remaining water will be used to thoroughly rinse the settled acids from the concentrate container into the rest of the mix. For a deep red oloroso sherry, add one gallon plus one quart of red grape concentrate to the primary fermenter. If you prefer to make a light fino sherry, use one gallon plus one quart of white grape concentrate. Pour the sugar solution into the primary fermenter.

To further enhance and round out the flavor, add a blend of banana flavor. Traditionally, the home wine maker has followed an old procedure found in most wine-making books which calls for boiling dried bananas in water for a period of time to release the flavors and essences. Unfortunately, most of the essential oils and flavors are boiled away using this procedure, leaving very little flavor to enhance the wine. The best method of blending in a banana flavor is also the easiest and least expensive: simply add a 1½-ounce bottle of Wagner's banana extract to the mix. This is a pure banana extract which retains all the natural aroma and volatile oils through distillation. It is available from specialty food shops and gourmet counters in major department stores across the country. This extract provides the roundness of flavor required of sherry and eliminates the racking and straining steps required when a pound or so of bananas are floating around in the wine as it ferments. After the banana flavoring has been stirred in, add four level teaspoons each of acid blend and nutrient.

Next, the fermentation is initiated using the Montrachet wine yeast. The flor-sherry yeast is not used at the beginning because it is a slow starter, requiring at least five days to become active. Since it is important to get the fermentation under way rapidly to prevent the juice from spoiling, the fast-acting Montrachet is used. Into a cup of warm water not exceeding 115°, pour a pack of Montrachet yeast and let it reactivate. When it has returned to the surface in the form of a creamy head, stir it thoroughly into the solution, and then into the wine mix. Cover the primary fermenter with a sheet of plastic and secure it with tape, although not too tightly. Let the wine remain in the primary fermenter for ten days. The active fermentation will normally be completed in seven days, and the majority of the yeast will settle out in the next three days.

The next step is the transfer of the wine to the secondary fermenter and the addition of the flor-sherry yeast. Since the flor requires an aerobic environment to form, the procedure for adding it is different from that used with standard wine yeast and requires careful attention until the flor finally forms. Following is the best procedure for achieving the all-important flor, but don't be concerned if it takes several weeks to become evident. Transfer the wine from the primary to the secondary fermenter. During the siphoning, fill a wide-necked quart jar two thirds full with some of the wine. Finish siphoning the wine. To reactivate the flor sherry yeast, pour one pack into a cup of warm water not exceeding 115°. When the yeast rises to the surface of the water in the cup in the form of the creamy head, do *not* stir it into solution. We want this yeast to float on the surface as much as possible so that it can have contact with the air. The purpose of the separate jar of wine is to give the flor a more aerobic environment than is attainable in the secondary fermenter, although the flor is introduced into both the jar and the fermenter at the same time. Using a teaspoon, scoop about one third of the creamy head from the cup and place it carefully on the surface of the wine in the jar, allowing some to coat the inside of the jar just above the surface of the wine. Place the jar where it will not be moved or shaken, and cover the top with a sheet of plastic. Do not seal with tape. Prior to adding the remaining creamy head of yeast to the secondary fermenter, agitate the wine vigorously with a spoon close to the surface. This will aerate the wine and increase the chance of flor formation. Carefully place the yeast on the surface. Do not top up the secondary fermenter prior to attaching the lock. The air space is required in making sherry. When attaching the lock, do not put water in it. Just put a small piece of cotton in the top to keep out dust. This will allow air to get through. Remove the lock from the fermenter and the plastic from the jar once each day and fan air into the two containers. This is necessary to allow the flor to form. It should take about two weeks for a slight film to become evident, although it may take several weeks. The film will become thicker until it forms a definite layer on the surface. If this layer forms first in the fermenter, all well and good. Usually, however, the jar of wine will produce the flor bloom first. If this is the case, scoop as much of the flor as possible into the secondary fermenter. Replace the cotton-filled lock and allow the sherry to ferment for at least six months, the amount of time required to produce true sherry flavor.

Siphon the wine carefully off the yeast layer into the primary fermenter, containing ½ teaspoon of ascorbic acid. Since there will also be a top layer of yeast, care should be taken that very little is siphoned with the wine. Note that fining solution is not added to sherry at the start of the secondary fermentation as is the case with other wines. Because of the longer secondary fermentation, the wine should clear quite well by itself. If it seems to need further clearing after the secondary fermentation, however, you can dissolve one half teaspoon of fining powder in a small amount of water heated to just below boiling and stir it into the wine after it has been siphoned into the primary fermenter. Now add 1½ fifth-size bottles of brandy. This will bring the alcohol content to about 16 percent and also enhance the flavor slightly. If your taste is for cream sherry, you can sweeten the whole batch at this point by dissolving four level cups of sugar in two cups of water heated on the stove and stirring the sugar solution into the wine. This will provide a uniform sweetness to each bottle. If you like dry sherry or various degrees of sweetness, simply bottle the sherry as you would regular wine and sweeten each bottle to taste prior to drinking. The sherry should be stored upright at room temperature for at least a month prior to drinking; the flavor is considerably improved if you age it six months in the bottle. Decant and chill before serving. It will not be necessary to shake the sherry to dissipate gases as is the case with regular wines. The gases were completely dissipated during the six months in the secondary fermenter.

To simplify the formation of the flor for your next batch of sherry, just start the new batch ten days prior to bottling the previous one. Scoop out a good portion of the flor formation and add it directly to the surface of the new batch after transferring it to the secondary fermenter. This way you will not need to start a new flor formation, and the flor will begin working right away.

If you prefer a sherry with a higher alcohol content, you can add either more brandy or vodka to the batch prior to bottling. Each additional 1½ bottles will add about one percent alcohol. There is no need to go beyond about 18 percent, however.

One thing should be kept in mind when making sherry with the flor-sherry yeast. It is very active and must be completely cleaned out of your equipment before making regular wine or it will re-form and take over the fermentation.

PROCEDURE OUTLINE

INGREDIENTS

3¾ U.S. gallons of water
4 level cups of sugar
  (2 pounds)
4 level teaspoons acid blend
4 level teaspoons nutrient
1 gallon plus 1 quart red or
  white grape concentrate
1 bottle Wagner's banana
  extract
Montrachet and flor-sherry
  yeast
½ teaspoon ascorbic acid
½ level teaspoon fining
  powder (optional)
1½ fifth-size bottles of brandy

EQUIPMENT

Rigid primary fermenter—
  7 gallons
Rigid secondary fermenter—
  5½ gallons
Large saucepan
Hydrometer
Extra-wide plastic sheet
Masking or Scotch tape
Measuring cup
Siphon unit
25 fifty-size bottles, tops
Quart-size jar

1. Fill carboy to 5 inches from top with cold water. Pour some of that water into large saucepan and heat. Pour in 4 cups of sugar and dissolve.

2. Add 4 level teaspoons each of acid blend and nutrient to primary fermenter. Transfer all but 1 quart of water from carboy to primary fermenter. Pour in sugar water from saucepan. Add concentrate, rinse its containers thoroughly with remaining water from carboy, and add to mix. Add banana extract.

3. Pour 1 pack of Montrachet yeast into 1 cup of warm water not exceeding 115°. When yeast forms a creamy foam on surface of water, stir thoroughly into solution, then stir into wine mix. Cover primary fermenter with sheet of plastic, seal with tape. Allow primary fermentation to continue for 10 days.

4. Siphon some of the wine into a quart-size Mason-type jar and remainder into carboy. Prepare flor-sherry yeast by pouring pack into 1 cup of warm water not exceeding 115°. When creamy head forms on surface of water in cup, transfer the yeast cream to the surface of wine in jar and carboy without stirring. Agitate wine in carboy prior to adding yeast. Cover jar with plastic sheet and fit lock to carboy without water in it. Put cotton in lock to keep out dust. Aerate both carboy and jar daily by fanning air into them. If flor forms first in jar, transfer it to surface of wine in carboy. Fit lock and let ferment for 6 months.

5. Siphon wine into primary fermenter containing ½ teaspoon ascorbic acid. Add 1½ fifth-size bottles of brandy. Sweeten if desired using 4 cups of sugar in solution. Siphon into standard fifth or quart bottles, seal, store upright at room temperature for at least 1 month. Decant, serve chilled. Flavor is much improved after aging 6 months.

Port

Port is a wine which was developed in Portugal by the English. If this seems a little odd, it is necessary to look at how port evolved from an ordinary wine to the well-known fortified dessert beverage of today. Politics had a great influence on the evolution of port wine. The British, during the seventeenth century, imported large amounts of wine, since the grape did not flourish in the climate and soil of England. Most British wine came from France, although a small amount was brought from Portugal. This state of affairs was soon reversed, however, when the English, in one of their perennial wars with the French, decided to cut down on the importation of French wine and signed a treaty with Portugal making it a principal supplier of wine to the British Isles. The English did not particularly care for the Portuguese wine at first. It was harsh compared to the French wines to which they had grown accustomed. In due time, the English wine merchants in Portugal, who controlled the wine trade, hit on the idea of adding brandy to the wine prior to the completion of fermentation. This would halt any further fermentation, causing the wine to be sweet as a result of the remaining unfermented grape sugars and giving it a character all its own, due to the blending of brandy with the wine. This suited the English palate, and port wine has enjoyed its place as one of the world's great dessert wines ever since. Interestingly, the Portuguese themselves do not consume much port. Since their climate is far warmer than England's, they prefer the original unfortified wines.

The two major types of port most popular in the United States are ruby and tawny. These are blends of several varieties of grape wine. The ruby is a fruity blend of young ports and has a deep ruby color. The tawny is also a blend of various ports, but these have been aged more, resulting in a less fruity bouquet and taste, and a lighter color.

A very good port can be made in the home. The procedure which follows is along the same lines as the one for regular wine. The fermentation will be quite rapid despite the additional sugars included in the ingredients.

PROCEDURE

You will need one gallon plus two quarts of red grape concentrate. Fill the secondary fermenter to a height of four inches from the top as the initial water measure. Transfer a quart of this water to a saucepan and all but about a quart to the primary fermenter. As in the regular wine section, this leftover water is used to thoroughly rinse out the acids which have settled in the concentrate containers. Dissolve two pounds of sugar in the water heated in the saucepan and pour into the primary fermenter. Add all the concentrate, four level teaspoons of nutrient, and two level teaspoons of acid blend. For blending purposes, add a 1½-ounce bottle of Wagner's banana extract. (See chapter on sherry.) The banana extract is required to round out the flavor; however, it will not impart a noticeable banana taste to the wine if added during this initial mixing stage. When all of these ingredients have been mixed thoroughly in the primary fermenter, the specific gravity will be approximately 1.110. This sugar level will give a final alcohol content of 15 percent. Unlike the regular wines, the final specific gravity of port will be 1.000.

Reactivate the Montrachet yeast in a cup of warm water not exceeding 115°. When the creamy head rises to the surface of the water in the cup, stir it completely into solution with a spoon and then into the wine mix in the primary fermenter. Tape a piece of plastic sheet over the primary fermenter, and let the wine ferment at room temperature. After seven or eight days of active fermentation, when the tumultuous stage has subsided, check the specific gravity of the wine. When it is approximately 1.000 to 1.005, transfer the wine to the secondary fermenter. Add one half level teaspoon of finings dissolved in hot water. If there is excessive air space left in the secondary fermenter after siphoning, top it up to just below the neck with water. Fill the fermentation lock to a depth of one half inch with water and attach it to the fermenter. Let the secondary fermentation continue for two months.

At the end of this time, siphon the wine carefully off the yeast layer into the primary fermenter, containing one half level teaspoon of ascorbic acid. The wine may be quite clear at this point, so be very careful not to suck up any of the yeast layer. Agitate the wine vigorously for several minutes with a long-handled spoon to dissipate the residual malo-lactic gases. Add 1½ bottles of brandy. The addition of brandy will enhance the flavor and increase the alcohol content to 16 percent by volume.

For a tawny port, dissolve three level cups of sugar in two cups of water heated on the stove, and add to the wine in the primary fermenter. For a regular port, dissolve four cups of sugar in two cups of water, and add to the wine. For a sweet ruby port, dissolve five cups of sugar in three cups of water and add to the wine. There will be no refermentation of the wine after adding the sugar because of the high alcohol content. Bottle and cap, using the method from the standard wine section. Age upright at room temperature for two months, although the peak flavor is not reached prior to six months of aging. Decant into a quart bottle, shake vigorously, and let it sit overnight in the refrigerator with the cap on loosely so that the port can breathe. Serve chilled.

PROCEDURE OUTLINE

INGREDIENTS	EQUIPMENT
1½ gallons Bear Mountain red grape concentrate	Rigid primary fermenter— 7 gallons
4 U.S. gallons of water	Rigid secondary fermenter—
4 level cups sugar (2 pounds)	5½ gallons
4 level teaspoons nutrient	Large saucepan
2 level teaspoons acid blend	Hydrometer
1 bottle Wagner's banana extract	Extra-wide plastic sheet
Montrachet active dry yeast	Masking or Scotch tape
½ level teaspoon fining powder	Measuring cup
½ level teaspoon ascorbic acid	Siphon unit
1½ fifth-size bottles of brandy	27 fifth-size bottles, tops

1. Fill carboy to 4 inches from top with cold water. Pour about 1 quart of that water into large saucepan and heat. Pour in 2 pounds of sugar and dissolve.
2. Add 4 level teaspoons of nutrient and 2 level teaspoons of acid blend to primary fermenter. Transfer all but 1 quart of water from carboy to primary fermenter. Pour in sugar water from saucepan. Add concentrate, rinse its container thoroughly with remaining water from carboy and add to mix. Add banana extract.
3. Pour 1 pack Montrachet yeast into 1 cup of warm water not exceeding 115°. When yeast forms a creamy foam on surface of water, stir thoroughly into solution, then pour into wine mix and stir. Cover primary fermenter with plastic sheet, seal with tape. Cover with cloth. Allow to ferment

until specific gravity reads approximately 1.000, usually 7 to 8 days.

4. Siphon wine into carboy. Dissolve fining powder in hot water and add during siphoning. Attach fermentation lock and age 2 months.

5. Siphon wine carefully off yeast layer into primary fermenter containing ½ level teaspoon ascorbic acid. Agitate several minutes with long-handled spoon to dissipate gases. Add 1½ bottles of brandy. For tawny port, add 3 level cups sugar completely dissolved in hot water. For regular port, add 4 level cups sugar. For rich ruby port, add 5 level cups sugar. Stir thoroughly. Siphon into bottles, seal as indicated in regular wine section. Store upright at room temperature at least 2 months. Peak flavor reached after 6 months of aging in bottle. Decant and serve chilled.

Champagne

Champagne is the most festive of all wines. Each bottle is filled with effervescent gaiety to match the spirit of the occasion for which it is opened. As wines go, champagne made a rather late arrival on the scene. A Benedictine monk, Dom Pérignon, is credited with inventing champagne in the later part of the seventeenth century. As the story goes, he was puttering around in the abbey wine cellar one evening when some bottles started bursting and corks began to fly. It seems that the good brothers had bottled their wine too soon and a spell of warm weather had caused the wine to referment as a result of the sugars remaining in the wine. After he had regained his wits, Brother Dom opened one of the remaining bottles and sampled it. His first remark after tasting the sparkling wine was "Oh, come quickly, I am drinking stars!" Whether these were his exact words is hard to confirm.

At any rate, they are a fitting enough tribute to the origin of the bubbly beverage. Dom Pérignon laid most of the groundwork and established most of the procedures which are still used in the production of fine champagne. He developed the art of blending various grapes to enhance the wine and to maintain consistency of taste.

Champagne is one wine that simply cannot be duplicated in the home, at least not the expensive French variety. The process of making champagne is a very long and exacting one. In France, it is made in the region historically called Champagne, with two varieties of grapes, the Pinot Noir, and the white Pinot. The grapes are harvested in the fall and are then hand-sorted, so that only the finest and ripest are used. The grapes are put into huge pressers which extract the juices, which are then run off into large casks. When the primary fermentation subsides, the casks are sealed. By this time, the cold winter weather has arrived and the yeast becomes inactive. In the spring, when warm weather reactivates the yeast, the remaining sugar level of the wine is checked. If it is below the desired level, pure cane sugar syrup is added. The wine is then transferred to bottles, which are sealed and stored upside down. The yeast works on the sugar in the sealed bottles to produce a little more alcohol and the all-important carbon dioxide which gives the wine its effervescence. Because of the renewed fermentation, a yeast deposit settles in the neck and on the cork.

The bottles are left to age for several years in this fashion. Periodically, workers give a sharp turn to each bottle to make sure that the yeast sediment falls to the very top of the neck, rather than clinging to the sides of the bottle. The next step is called the dégorgement. For the champagne to be clear, the yeast sediment must be removed. This is done by partially freezing the neck of the bottle. The cork is then released, and the frozen plug of sediment is expelled under pressure. The small amount of wine lost in this procedure is replaced by other champagne kept for this purpose. A new cork is placed in the bottle and wired down. The champagne is then aged further in the bottle prior to shipping.

As you can see, these are quite complicated procedures which take great skill and patience, not to mention the use of the freshly picked grapes from special regions required for a good champagne. While it is difficult to turn out a true champagne at home, you can make a good closely related sparkling wine such as sparkling burgundy or one resembling the popular Cold Duck. The following procedure employs the same method to carbonate the wine as was used originally in France prior to the development of the dégorgement. The finished wine will be a robust red sparkling wine, with sugar added to make it either sweet or semisweet.

PROCEDURE

Make up a five-gallon batch of wine using the procedure described for regular wine. Two quarts each of red and white concentrate are excellent. For a more robust sparkling burgundy, use only the red. The Cold Duck concentrate can be used if you prefer a less mellow wine with a sharper character. The only change in procedure required in the initial preparation of the wine is to use only two pounds of sugar in the ingredients. This will produce a wine with an alcohol content of about 10 percent. It is important to have a lower alcohol content in the wine initially so that the refermentation is not hampered later on. After the wine has aged in the secondary fermenter for the required thirty days, continue through step five of the procedure outline (page 64), which calls for transferring the wine back to the primary fermenter, adding ascorbic acid, and stirring vigorously.

At this point it is necessary to add sugar to the wine in the primary fermenter, along with champagne yeast, so that refermentation can begin. Mix three-fifths of a measuring cup (midway between one-half and two-thirds of a cup) of household sugar with a cup of water in a saucepan and heat. Stir until the sugar is totally dissolved into solution; then pour it into the wine and stir thoroughly, so that it is evenly distributed throughout the wine.

Prepare a pack of Universal Foods dry champagne yeast by pouring it into a cup of warm water not exceeding 115°. When the creamy head rises and covers the surface of the water, stir it thoroughly so that all the yeast lumps are mixed into solution. Pour this yeast solution directly into the wine and stir thoroughly. Since the champagne yeast is cultured to tolerate a higher level of alcohol than the Montrachet, it will have no trouble in stimulating the wine to referment, even in the 10 percent alcohol environment.

Siphon the wine into standard-size champagne bottles. *Do not under any circumstances use any other type of bottle!* Beer bottles and soft-drink bottles are not made to withstand the pressure and they will explode, sometimes with very painful consequences. Use only those types of champagne bottles which accept the plastic champagne cork. These are easy to obtain from restaurants and hotels, especially after a wedding reception. The stoppers must be wired down. Standard champagne bottle wires can be obtained at nominal cost from the various wine makers' supply outlets. When the bottles have been sealed and wired, store them upright at room temperature for two months. This will give the yeast sufficient time to convert all the residual sugar and will allow the wine to settle and clear. After two months, hold a bottle up to the light to check its clarity. If the light casts a sharp image through the bottle, it has cleared. If there is still some slight haze above the yeast layer, let it age another few weeks.

The next step is to transfer the wine into another bottle. When you are ready to begin transferring the wine, make up a sugar solution by heating in a saucepan two parts sugar to one part water. Stir until the sugar is completely in solution. You will also need some stabilizer tablets. These are added to each bottle so that the yeast is inhibited, thus preventing any fermentation of the sweetening sugar. The stabilizer tablets usually consist of sorbic acid, a fruit acid which discourages yeast growth. They are available through most wine makers' supply firms and are usually added at the rate of one per bottle; this depends on the size of the tablet, however, so follow the directions on the packet carefully.

Transfer the wine from the aging bottle to another champagne bottle leaving behind the yeast sediment which formed on the bottom during the refermentation. To avoid losing the carbonation, chill the wine and the bottle to which it will be transferred. Carbon dioxide gas is retained in a cold solution, whereas, in a warm solution, it quickly dissipates. Ideally, you would need twenty-five extra champagne bottles, to equal the number from which the wine is being poured, but for practical reasons you will need only five extra ones. Also necessary is a freezer chest which can accommodate several full and empty bottles. The bottles are usually cooled and transferred five at a time, due to space limitations in most freezer chests. Place the full and empty bottles upright in the freezer and let them cool until the wine is just above freezing temperature. When this stage is reached, remove the plastic cork from the bottle and decant it slowly into the empty bottle, being careful not to disturb the yeast layer on the bottom. Try not to bubble the wine at the neck as it is being poured. A funnel will facilitate pouring. Let the wine run into the other bottle at a slant so that it is not agitated during pouring. Set aside the first bottle of transferred champagne to top up the rest of the bottles. Add the stabilizer tablet, or the amount called for on the instruction label, to each bottle. These must be crushed and dissolved in a little water. Add one ounce of sugar syrup to each bottle, or two ounces if a sweeter wine is desired. Transfer the wine into the bottle and top up to the standard height using the wine from the first bottle. Seal the bottles with the plastic corks and wire down. Let them age at least one month, upright, at room temperature. The day after transferring the wine, when it has had time to warm up, shake the bottle several times to allow the sugar solution to mix thoroughly throughout the wine. Prior to serving the sparkling wine, chill it well.

PROCEDURE OUTLINE

1. Follow procedure outline for regular wine through step five, using only 2 pounds of sugar.
2. Dissolve ⅗ cup of sugar in 1 cup water, heated in a saucepan. Add sugar solution to wine and stir thoroughly.
3. Reactivate 1 pack of Universal Foods dry champagne yeast in 1 cup of water not exceeding 115°. Stir the reactivated yeast completely into solution, and pour into the wine, stirring thoroughly.
4. Siphon wine into standard champagne bottles with plastic corks and wire down. Store upright for 2 months.
5. Chill several bottles of the wine and the empty bottles to just above freezing.
6. Make up sugar syrup using 2 parts sugar to 1 part water, dissolved by heating in a saucepan and stirring.
7. Crush and dissolve 1 stabilizer tablet in a small amount of water and add to each empty bottle. Remove the plastic cork and carefully pour the chilled wine from the aging bottle to the chilled empty champagne bottle. Set aside the first bottle of sparkling wine to be used in topping up the others. No sugar syrup is added to this bottle. Add 1 ounce of sugar syrup to each succeeding bottle of wine and top up to the standard height with wine from the first bottle. If a sweeter wine is desired, use 2 ounces of syrup.
8. Soften the plastic corks in hot water and insert in the bottles. Wire down the corks and store at room temperature. After 1 day shake each bottle to mix the sweetener. Age upright for at least 1 month. Serve chilled.

Fruit Wines

In addition to grape wine concentrates the wine makers' supply firms carry a wide assortment of other fruit wines, such as peach, cherry, apricot, etc. These can be made by the same procedures used for regular wine. As with grape concentrates, these fruit concentrates come in gallon sizes, although the sugar content may differ from that of the grape. This variation can be corrected by adding household sugar with the use of the hydrometer to bring the sugar level up to the ideal range of 1.080–1.085. Pour the gallon of fruit concentrate in 4½ gallons of water in the primary fermenter and take a hydrometer reading. If it is below the ideal range, simply scoop up some of the juice, heat it in a saucepan, and dissolve sugar in it. Each pound of sugar will raise the specific gravity reading approximately .005. If the reading was 1.070 prior to adding sugar, for example, you would need to dissolve about 2½ pounds of sugar in some of the juice to bring the level to the ideal height. Once this is achieved, follow the procedure outline for regular wine, using Montrachet yeast.

The fermentation will proceed as indicated for grape wine, although the fruit wines generally do not need to age as long as grape wine. For some of the lighter fruit flavors, such as apricot and peach, which contain very little tannin, it may be necessary to add about one level teaspoon of powdered tannin with the initial ingredients. This will aid the gelatin in clearing the wine later on. Tannin is available through wine makers' supply firms.

Liqueurs

Liqueurs are a rather recent development, historically speaking. While beer and wine have been with us since the earliest period of recorded history, liqueurs have been around only for the last two thousand years or so. The obvious reason for their late arrival is that liqueurs are not a natural product of nature. Imagine a scene from the dawn of civilization in which groups of our distant ancestors gathered wild grains or picked clusters of grapes and stored them in damp depressions in the backs of their caves for consumption during the long winter months. Water would trickle in from among the rocks and fill these storage holes. Fermentation would take place from ever-present wild yeasts and lo and behold, our Cro-Magnon friends would end up with either a community beer keg or a wine cellar with no effort on their part. Archaeologists have discovered several caves with residues of beer and wine fermentation, so it is quite easy to imagine a scene in which a group of raucous cavemen make periodic trips to the back of the cave to scoop out a portion of fermenting wort or must in their crude earthen cups and return slightly drunk to fight for their place around the fire, but one is hard put to try to visualize one of these hairy individuals sitting around a campfire sipping Crème de Menthe. This came later, much later, when his mind developed to the point where he was able to invent that most amazing contraption, a still.

One of the first references to the use of liqueur was made by Cicero (106–43 B.C.), the Roman philosopher. He spoke of a popular drink of the period distilled from rose petals. Merchants and adventurers returning from the East spoke of a fiercely powerful drink popular with the Arabs which was distilled from the juice of fermented dates; it was known as *al-kuhl,* from which the word "alcohol" is derived. It was not until the Middle Ages, however, that liqueurs came into general use. They were developed by the alchemists, monks, and sorcerers of that medieval period. These men were looking for potions that would turn common metals to gold, and others that would preserve youth. They didn't succeed in these goals, but they did manage to produce some interesting liqueurs or cordials. The term cordial is for practical purposes synonymous with liqueur. It comes from the word "*cordialis,*" which means "of the heart." Quite appropriate, since these first liqueurs were used as medicines and aphrodisiacs. The medicinal qualities of some liqueurs are well established, especially those made from coriander, caraway seeds, and various roots and herbs.

France is the source of most of the finest liqueurs available today. The types are quite varied, and the number of flavors is limited only by the variety of plants and fruits available which have a palatable taste. Liqueurs are divided into two categories generally, those made with plants and those made with fruits. There are three methods used to produce liqueurs: infusion, distillation, and the adding of essential oils and flavors.

Most fruit liqueurs are made with the infusion and distillation methods. The fruit is left to steep in brandy or neutral grain spirits for a period of time to extract the flavor and aroma. When the liquid has been drawn off, the remaining fruit pulp is distilled to extract any remaining oils and flavor constituents. These are then added to the rest of the liqueur to give it more flavor and character. Sugar is added to attain the desired amount of sweetness, and the liqueur is then aged for mellowness.

Plant liqueurs are made using the distillation method. The flavors of the plants, herbs, or seeds cannot be effectively extracted by infusion. They are usually softened for a day or two in spirits and are then placed in a vat so that a stream of brandy or other spirits can flow over them to extract the flavor. The whole amount is distilled out to extract all remaining flavors after several months. Sugar is added and the liqueur is aged to make it mellow. Unlike the fruit liqueurs, the plant liqueurs turn out colorless. Some, like the green Crème de Menthe, have coloring added to increase their appeal.

The third method of making liqueurs is to simply add the essential oils or flavoring extract to either brandy or neutral grain spirits, although this flavoring may have been made separately by the processes shown above. This is the process used to make liqueurs at home.

For many years, Europeans have been making liqueurs at home using extracts prepared for this purpose by several overseas firms. The largest and most famous of these extract companies is the T. Noirot firm of Nancy, France, which has been making liqueur extracts for home use for over eighty years. Since their products are now available in this country through most wine makers' supply outlets, the procedures for making liqueurs will deal with this particular brand.

It is very easy to make your own liqueurs. The complicated processes of extracting flavors and recapturing essential oils have already been accomplished, and all that is required to make the liqueur is to add the bottle of extract and sugar to vodka or brandy and serve. No aging is required, so those liqueurs can be served the day they are made. Besides the fun of serving a beverage made in the home, there are other advantages to making your own liqueurs. With forty liqueur flavors to choose from, you have a much greater variety than can be found in most liquor stores; indeed, many of the liqueurs are not even sold commercially in this country. For the majority of the liqueurs the cost is much less than buying them already made up. The price of a bottle of the extract to make up one quart is around a dollar. The cost of just under a fifth of inexpensive vodka or brandy brings the total cost of making a quart of liqueur to under four dollars for any of the forty varieties. The cost of the commercial product ranges from four to ten dollars a fifth, depending on the type and brand. Finally, the taste is equal to the commercial variety and, with some of the flavors, is decidedly superior to the store-bought counterpart. Following is the procedure for making liqueurs.

The extracts come in three-fourth-ounce bottles—sufficient quantity to make up one quart of liqueur. The only equipment you will need is a small saucepan, a measuring cup, a funnel, and a quart bottle. Do not use a fifth-size bottle or the flavor will be too concentrated and unbalanced. After choosing the particular type of liqueur you wish to make up, check page 105 to see whether it is classified as sweet, medium, or dry. For sweet liqueurs, mix 1⅓ measuring cups of sugar and two-thirds of a cup of water in the saucepan. Heat and stir until the sugar is completely dissolved into solution. Pour some vodka or brandy, depending on what you use as the base, into the clean quart bottle; then add the bottle of liqueur extract. Using a funnel, pour in the sugar solution while it is hot. If it cools down, it is very difficult to pour. The reason for pouring some of the vodka or brandy into the quart bottle initially is to prevent to bottle from cracking, which could happen if the hot sugar syrup were poured into the empty bottle. When the sugar solution has been added, fill the bottle to the standard height with vodka or brandy. Shake vigorously. It is necessary to shake more thoroughly when mixing extracts which contain a high quantity of essential oils such as Curaçao and Reverendine, to ensure a thorough mixing of the extract. Put the liqueur in the refrigerator for an hour or two, so that it can cool down from the hot sugar syrup. When it has reached room temperature or lower, it is ready to serve.

For medium liqueurs, follow the same procedure, except that only two-thirds of a cup of sugar is mixed with one-third of a cup of water to make up the required sugar solution. For dry liqueurs no sugar is used. Paste-on labels which identify the particular type of liqueur being made are included with each bottle of extract. For the professional touch, you can put the label on a distinctive liqueur bottle and transfer most of the liqueur to it for serving purposes. People's tastes in liqueurs vary widely. My preference in the home-made liqueurs is for the Crème de Cacao, the Moka, which is a distinctively light coffee liqueur, and Curaçao, all served chilled. On the following pages is a description of all the liqueurs which can be made at home.

Origin and Description of Liqueurs and Brandies

The following is a list of the types of liqueurs that can be made at home, along with a description of the ingredients and origin of some of the flavors. The names and spellings of the various liqueurs are those used by the makers of the extracts and may not be familiar to those of you who have not made liqueurs at home.

AMERICAN GROG

Developed in northern countries with a cold, humid climate. It is usually drunk cold, as are other liqueurs, but in wintertime it can be served hot with a twist of lemon.

ANISETTE

Typically French liqueur, well known in Europe and becoming popular around the world. Produced as either white or green liqueur. It has digestive properties due to several ingredients: fennel, aniseed, and coriander. Pliny, the Roman naturalist, attributed to this liqueur the double powers of inducing sleep and giving eternal youth to faces.

APRICOT

Made principally from apricots but containing essences of other fruits grown in the Rhone Valley and on Provence hillsides.

BANANA

One of four liqueurs known as island liqueurs, the others being Cocoa, Moka, and vanilla. These have been enjoyed for over a century and are characterized by a fine, smooth taste. They are dessert liqueurs, very mild, rather heavy, but not too strong. Their origins are the islands of Martinique, Guadeloupe, and Barbados. The banana liqueur is made principally from extract of banana in which the volatile oils have been retained.

BLACKBERRY

Made from a marinade and infusion of wild fruit picked in the Vosges forest in northeast France. These fruits, which are ripened in the shadow of tall pines, have a unique character.

BLACK CURRANT

A well-known liqueur made by marinating and distilling fruit grown on the Burgundy and Lorraine slopes of France, where this shrub thrives.

CAFE SPORT

A mild-flavored liqueur with hint of coffee, enhanced by a blend of almond and vanilla.

CHERRY BRANDY

A popular liqueur, which originated in Scandinavia. It is one of the more expensive liqueurs when purchased commercially. Cherry brandy is made from a marinade of wild cherries with the pits and other juices to enhance the flavor. It is a heavy liqueur.

CREME DE CACAO

In my opinion one of the most delicious cordials. The flavor is obtained from the cacao (cocoa) bean and the vanilla bean. The extract contains a greater amount of vanilla than is used in most commercial varieties of crème de cacao, which seems to greatly enhance the flavor.

DANTZIG

A German liqueur (*Danziger Goldwasser*). The flavor is obtained from the peels of oranges, with other spices and herbs blended in. This liqueur is unique in that it has tiny gold flakes floating in it. They are harmless when consumed.

DRY GIN

A brandy made from juniper berries and branches which grow wild in Mediterranean countries, the Alps, and the Caucasus. As the name implies, this is not a sweet liqueur, as no sugar is used in preparing it.

FRENCH YELLOW BRANDY

A mixture of fruit and plants prepared with brandy to give a taste similar to Cognac.

GENEPY

A spicy, aromatic liqueur with a licorice taste, Genepy originated in Italy. It is obtained from Alpine wormwood or artemisia. The extract is made from a type of dwarf artemisia which grows only at high elevations in the rocky clefts of the Alps. It is considered a stimulant much appreciated by mountaineers.

GREEN CONVENT

A plant liqueur with a spicy, aromatic taste. This, along with Yellow Convent, is a very popular liqueur in France.

GREEN MINT

Made from the well-known English plant. Only one of the numerous varieties of mint, peppermint, is used in liqueur making. The liqueur has a tangy flavor.

KIRSCH

A very popular brandy in eastern France and the Black Forest region of Germany. Made from the black cherry distilled with the pits, which lend a slight almond taste to it.

KUMMEL

First made in Holland. Later, the Russians developed a taste for it, and they have been the principal producers over the years. It is made with caraway seeds. Its strong flavor and composition make it a powerful digestive stimulant.

MARASCHINO

Of southern European origin, well known and very popular in Yugoslavia. It is made from a small variety of cherry similar to the French wild cherry.

MOKA

A coffee liqueur. It is much lighter in body than most domestic and imported coffee liqueurs found commercially, yet the taste is quite pleasing.

ORANGE BRANDY

A delicious, typically French liqueur made from bitter oranges, cocoa beans, and vanilla tincture. Besides being a good after-dinner drink, it is also ideal for flavoring certain desserts and pastries.

ORANGE RED CURACAO

A tonic and stimulating liqueur of Dutch origin obtained by distilling orange peel and green bigarade oranges from the island of Curaçao.

ORANGE TRIPLE DRY

Also known as white Curaçao or Triple Sec. It is similar to Orange Red Curaçao but is traditionally higher in alcohol content and should be made with one-hundred-proof vodka.

PEACH

Obtained from fresh and aged peaches.

PEAR

Made from a pear specially developed in the Valais area of Switzerland for use in liqueurs. It was first used to make a brandy, then became the principal fruit in a sweet liqueur.

RASPBERRY

As with the Blackberry, this liqueur is made from an infusion of wild fruit gathered from the Vosges forest in France. This is a sweeter and heavier liqueur than the Blackberry.

RATAFIA

Also known as wine makers' liqueur, as it is made from gray wine. It is similar to Cherry Brandy, although it has a characteristic woody taste imparted from the barrels used to age the wine.

REVERENDINE

Made from a marinade and infusion of plants and herbs. It was developed many years ago by the Trappist monks of Sainte Vanne in Lorraine, France, and is reputed to have great medicinal value for stomach ailments.

SLOE GIN

Made from an infusion of sloeberries. In France the sloe is popular in the form of a sweet liqueur known as Prunelle. In Britain and the United States, it is preferred in a drier form. This particular extract is a harmonious mixture of Prunelle and gin which can be served straight or used as a cocktail mixture.

STRESS

Originated in Italy. It is an infusion of various plants with spices added to enhance the flavor.

SWEDISH PUNCH

A spicy Scandinavian liqueur made from vanilla tincture, coffee and cocoa infusions, with lemon and cinnamon spirits.

SWEET ALMONDS

Made from the extract of sweet almonds, this liqueur was originally developed on the island of Martinique, but is now also made in the south of France, where almond trees grow in abundance.

TANGERINE

A very popular liqueur in France, Spain, and Italy. It has a very pleasing taste, derived from tangerines grown on the island of Sicily.

VANILLA

A mild, rather heavy dessert liqueur, made from the extract of the vanilla bean.

VERBENA

Originated in the Auvergne and Provence regions of France. It is made from the leaves of the ornamental vervain plant grown in Spain, Central America, and France.

WHITE MINT

Also called Crème de Menthe. It is identical to the Green Mint except that it has had no coloring added.

YELLOW CONVENT

Similar in taste to the Green Convent. Traditionally, the Yellow Convent should have a lower alcohol content than the Green. This is accomplished by mixing the yellow with eighty-proof vodka and the green with one-hundred-proof vodka.

YELLOW PLUM

Originally an Oriental fruit which was brought to France by crusaders returning from Palestine in the Middle Ages. The particular plum used in this extract is grown near Nancy, France, where the iron-rich soil is quite favorable for this small golden fruit.

YELLOW PRUNELLA

Made from the fruit of the wild sloe. The sloeberries grow on thorny bushes which thrive in uncultivated areas. The sloe is a bitter berry which can only be picked after the first frosts.

YELLOW GENEPY

Similar to Genepy. It has a distinctive yellow color and is like a popular commercial liqueur imported from Italy.

Classification of Liqueurs

SWEET
American Grog
Apricot
Banana
Black currant
Café Sport
Cocoa
Green Anisette
Green Mint
Maraschino
Moka
Peach
Pear
Raspberry
Swedish Punch
Sweet Almonds
Tangerine
Vanilla
White Anisette
White Mint
Yellow Plum
Yellow Prunella

MEDIUM
Blackberry
Cherry Brandy
Dantzig
Genepy
Green Convent
Kümmel
Orange Brandy
Orange Red Curaçao
Orange Triple Dry
Ratafia
Reverendine
Sloe Gin
Stress
Verbena
Yellow Convent
Yellow Genepy

BRANDIES (no sugar syrup)
Dry Gin
French Yellow Brandy
Kirsch

Beadle's Champagne Cider

Cider is a delicious, refreshing beverage made from the juice of apples. Good hard cider was a staple in most American households until around the turn of the century, but it is rarely seen today. The type of cider I'm referring to is not the sweet apple juice found in grocery stores, but good, hard, carbonated cider which has been blessed by the kiss of the yeast. It is a beverage with only a moderate alcohol content, usually no more than that of beer. In the old days, apples were crushed and squeezed in a press to release the juices, which were run into wooden barrels to begin fermentation. Some was consumed during the early stages of fermentation. It is during this period that it is at its best. Cider is the only beverage that is palatable during the fermentation. After fermentation was finished and all the sugars converted to alcohol and carbon dioxide gas, the dry cider was either bottled and drunk as a dry apple wine, which was not particularly tasty, or more likely it was distilled into applejack, a fiercely potent beverage with the same alcohol content as whiskey. Not wishing to incur the wrath of the Internal Revenue Service, I shall refrain from a discussion of the techniques of making applejack; besides, sparkling cider is a much more delicious beverage. Some people even refer to it as apple champagne. It is an extremely easy drink to make, requires no specialized equipment, and is ready three days after mixing it up. It is a drink well suited to mealtimes or anytime, but it is a particularly festive addition to Thanksgiving and Christmas dinners.

To make apple cider you will need an ordinary glass gallon jug, a roll of Saran Wrap, a small rubber band, some Montrachet wine yeast, and some apple juice. Do not buy apple juice or cider which is already made up in gallon or quart sizes in the grocery store. It is too weak to make good cider. The best method is to buy the frozen apple concentrate which comes in six-ounce cans similar to frozen orange juice. Let it thaw out, and add four cans to the gallon jug. Pour in eleven cans of water, using one of the empty apple concentrate cans. You will notice that this is a higher concentration of apple juice than the directions on the can indicate, but this is how you get good cider. Mix about one-third pack of Montrachet wine yeast in a small cup of warm water as indicated in the regular wine procedure. Add the yeast to the jug of apple juice and shake it once to allow the yeast solution to dissipate throughout the juice. Place a piece of Saran Wrap over the jug and secure it tightly over the top by doubling the rubber band over the neck. This will act as a low pressure valve through which the carbon dioxide can pass without letting air enter. It will also create enough positive pressure in the jug so that the cider will become effervescent. Let the jug sit for two days at room temperature. Fermentation will begin in a day, and a slight head may develop. After the second day of fermentation, put the jug in the refrigerator to cool. Wait one more day, and the apple cider is ready to drink. The jug is kept in the refrigerator because the cider tastes best when it is cold and because carbon dioxide is retained to a much greater degree in cold liquid than in warm. The cold air and the Saran Wrap covering will keep the cider fully carbonated like a bubbly champagne, even though the top is not sealed tightly with a cap or cork. (Never cap the jug or it will blow up like a bomb!)

The fermentation will continue at a slow rate in the cold air of the refrigerator, and removing the cover to pour out a glass from time to time will not affect the carbonation. The cider will be cloudy and smell yeasty, but the taste will be delicious. It should be served in heavy glass beer mugs which have been placed in the freezer prior to filling. When the cider is poured into the mugs directly from the jug, it will bubble and form a head just like a lively champagne. The jug can be kept in the refrigerator for two weeks and longer, during this time the cider will become increasingly dry as the sugars slowly ferment out. After two weeks the carbonation will decrease, but it will still be sufficient for those of you who prefer to wait and drink a less sweet cider. (Personally, I don't think many will wait this long. Most people around my area who have made up this cider finish it after two days in the refrigerator!)

In writing this book, I have tried to provide a detailed yet easy-to-follow guide to making quality wines and liqueurs. At the same time, I have sought to eliminate all of the errors and potential problems formerly encountered by the home wine maker. The response by the public to these procedures and recipes has been most gratifying. In the past several years, home wine making has steadily increased and continues to do so at a surprising rate. Many wine-making and wine-tasting clubs are being formed around the country, and as publicity in the field increases, more people become interested in this fascinating hobby. It wouldn't surprise me if in the next few years a bubbling vessel of fermenting wine becomes a common scene in most households as it was in the last century. I hope you all experience the same enjoyment as I have in turning out fine beverages in the home.

Equipment Supplies

The following components make up the standard home fermentation kit, which can be used to prepare all the wine recipes in this book.

1 heavy-duty polyethylene primary fermenter
1 heavy-duty polyethylene secondary fermenter (5½ U.S. gallons)
1 fermentation lock and inert stopper
1 precision fermentation hydrometer and jar
1 siphon unit
1 long-handled bottle brush
Montrachet active dry yeast
dried fermentation yeast
nutrient
acid blend
ascorbic acid
fining powder

For information on obtaining a complete fermentation kit, along with grape concentrates and other wine-making supplies, contact:

Specialty Products International, Ltd.
Box 784
Chapel Hill, North Carolina 27514
Telephone: 919 929-4277